MW01612047

Many Ibantes

Tyoapul

07/08/19

BUNDLE OF JOY

Exploring the Blessings of Reflection

Donald Tyoapine Komboh, PhD

WESTBOW
PRESS®
A DIVISION OF THOMAS NELSON
& ZONDERVAN

Copyright © 2019 Donald Tyoapine Komboh, PhD.

All rights reserved. No part of this book may be used or reproduced by any means, graphic, electronic, or mechanical, including photocopying, recording, taping or by any information storage retrieval system without the written permission of the author except in the case of brief quotations embodied in critical articles and reviews.

This book is a work of non-fiction. Unless otherwise noted, the author and the publisher make no explicit guarantees as to the accuracy of the information contained in this book and in some cases, names of people and places have been altered to protect their privacy.

Scripture quotations are from New Revised Standard Version Bible, copyright © 1989 National Council of the Churches of Christ in the United States of America. Used by permission. All rights reserved worldwide.

WestBow Press books may be ordered through booksellers or by contacting:

WestBow Press
A Division of Thomas Nelson & Zondervan
1663 Liberty Drive
Bloomington, IN 47403
www.westbowpress.com
1 (866) 928-1240

Because of the dynamic nature of the Internet, any web addresses or links contained in this book may have changed since publication and may no longer be valid. The views expressed in this work are solely those of the author and do not necessarily reflect the views of the publisher, and the publisher hereby disclaims any responsibility for them.

Any people depicted in stock imagery provided by Getty Images are models, and such images are being used for illustrative purposes only.
Certain stock imagery © Getty Images.

ISBN: 978-1-9736-6231-0 (sc)
ISBN: 978-1-9736-6233-4 (hc)
ISBN: 978-1-9736-6232-7 (e)

Library of Congress Control Number: 2019907121

Print information available on the last page.

WestBow Press rev. date: 06/10/2019

To the staff and students of St. Paul's College Seminary, Gbarnga, Liberia. Their affection and love are truly legendary.

Imprimatur: Most Rev. Jerome Lewis Zeigler
President: Catholic Bishop Conference of Liberia
Archbishop: Catholic Diocese of Monrovia, Liberia
Nihil obstat.
Very Rev. Fr. Dare Peter Ebidero
Vicar General, Catholic Diocese of Kano, Nigeria
Censor Deputatus

Foreword

S

T. PAUL TEACHES and reminds us that God, through the Spirit, gives a variety of gifts after services and activities to us. These are to be used for the common good (cf. 1 Corinthians 12:4–11). St. Peter likewise advises, "Like good stewards of the manifold grace of God serve one another with whatever gift each of you has received" (cf. 1 Peter 4:10–11). It is desirable and necessary, in all honesty and sincerity, to discern and know our specific gifts and grace from God and use them to serve good and humanity to edify them and lead them to God, not for self-indulgence or to puff ourselves up (see 1 Corinthians 8:1). That we are able to or enabled to know our gifts and use them well for the salvation of the souls and the glory of God, the Giver, we should always give thanks to God. It follows that to commend and to encourage one another in the proper use of our gifts and talents is important. It is, therefore, in this vein that I present to you this collection and commend Fr. Donald Komboh for publishing his reflections on the liturgical readings of the Mass over a period of time. You will observe that it does not serially follow the liturgical calendar (Ordo). This is understandable since he gave these reflections on the days the horarium had him presiding at the Eucharistic celebration in the seminary community (a place I am quite used to from my days in formation in the seminary). Again, as he says himself, the reader should be mindful of this context while reading and reflecting on these shared homilies.

This is not, however, to imply that the lessons therein cannot be applied to other situations in the life of a Christian. In the Word of God, there is always something for everyone and every situation because this Word is a living, dynamic, and active Word. It is, as Paul attests, "useful for teaching, for reproof, for correction, and for training in righteousness, so that everyone who belongs to God may be proficient, equipped for every good work" (2 Timothy 3:16). His thoughts are, no doubt, not exhaustive of the points raised or that could be raised, but they can lead to further thoughts and developments, all in an effort to apply the message to the life of both the user and the assembly the user would have to address. For this, I pray and hope. Thank you and well done, Fr. Donald, for the effort in putting down these reflections in a book and more so for scripting your reflections before they are shared with fellow worshipers—a practice and discipline all preachers of the Word of God should do and cultivate.

Most Rev. Dr. Charles Michaels Hammawa
Catholic Bishop of Jalingo Diocese
Taraba State, Nigeria

Acknowledgments

WORDS AREN'T ENOUGH to render my gratitude. I must say a lot has been put into making these reflections a reality. I am indeed grateful to so many who have ensured that these reflections see the light of day. I have so many to thank: the student community of St. Paul's College Seminary, its staff, and well-wishers who we have shared so much, especially when we prayed together. They remain, in all honesty, a mighty inspiration. I have the benefit of so many accomplished authors whose work I have quoted from and whose materials I have used. I am highly indebted to them.

I want to thank in a special way my brother, mentor, friend, and inspiration, Very Rev. Fr. Peter Dare Ebidero, who took an interest in this manuscript and ensured that it went to press and saw the light of day. My indebtedness also includes Frs. Faustinus Ike Ugwuanyi (Nsukka Diocese), Ferdinand Ihiekire (Archdiocese of Owerri), and Steve Udo (Ikot Ekpene Diocese), with whom I have shared so much in the seminary. Also, my gracious thanks go to Frs. Boniface Golo Tye, Martin Durham, and Very Rev. Fr. Francis Kofi Lyall, our highly esteemed rector. Let me not fail to mention Frs. Peter Alamaior Paase, MSP, and Tony Boweh of the Sacred Heart Cathedral, Monrovia. Importantly, I am grateful to His grace, Most Rev. Lewis Ziegler, Archbishop of the Catholic Archdiocese of Monrovia, for his extraordinary show of patience and kindness. Similarly, I would like to thank Very Rev. Fr. Chris Brenan, SMA, Apostolic Administrator of the Catholic Diocese of Gbarnga, Bong County, and Very Rev. Fr. Melvin Nyati Gaye,

Apostolic Administrator of the Catholic Diocese of Cape Palmas, Harper, Maryland County.

Srs. Patience Payne, Amelia Ade Wallace, and Emilia Wreh, all of the Congregation of the Holy Family, are owed my special thanks for constantly believing in me. Thank you also to Felicity Fanon and Tatigirl Nyama of the Calamites order and Ms. Michelle Candy Browne. May the good Lord bless you all. My publishers have done a great job, and they deserve special mention here too. Soji Sosanya and his crew in Lagos, Abeokuta, and Kano, you were all wonderful. Thank you. To my immediate and extended family members, I miss you all, but your prayers have been most helpful. Miss Prudence Madu and friends, including associates Macathony, Onyi, and Tayo, you have been such a blessing to me, and I think you too deserve special mention here.

I must not forget to include a special thanks to my bishop, Most Rev. Dr. Charles Michaels Hammawa, the Catholic Bishop of Jalingo Diocese, Taraba State, Nigeria, who at very short notice, agreed to do the foreword for this work; his brilliance and professionalism are unmatched. Thank you, my lord. I am grateful to a host of others around the west coast of Africa: from Sierra Leone, the Archbishop of Freetown and Bo, Most Rev. Dr. Edward Temba Charles; his vicar general, Very Fr. Joseph Kamada; Fr. Peter Odoh Konteh, our National Caritas Coordinator; Fr. Henry Aruna, National Director, PMS and ITBCABIC; Secretary General Fr. Charles Campbell, our spiritual director in the seminary, St. Paul's Major Seminary, Reagent, Freetown; Very Rev. Fr. Vincent Davis, the administrator of the Sacred Heart Cathedral; Fr. Tony Smart Nabie; and the Josephite Community in Freetown, Sierra Leone. There are a host of others too numerous to mention. I love you all and thank you.

In the Gambia, thank you to Most Rev Dr. Robert Ellison, Catholic Diocese of Banjul; Fr. Joseph Karl Gomez; Fr. Michael Gomez, CSSP; Fr. Ben, MBA, MSP; Fr. Bruno Toupan; Fr. Joseph Kabo; and Fr. Lopez. My appreciation for all your love. In my few visits to the Gambia, you have been most gracious with your time and all. May the good Lord bless you all. All mistakes and omissions remain mine.

A Word for Our Readers.

THIS SET OF reflections makes no pretense to be the most scholarly work. Indeed, a few scholarly objections can be raised. However, these reflections are guided by the fact of prayer and are drawn from the act of prayer itself. The language, although it may sometimes appear technical, is against the background of a student community. The language use is focused but is very inclusive. I hope that our readers will understand what we are about and spare a thought for prayer anytime they approach this work. All the chapters treat various themes and a thread runs through the work. The underlying thought is to enrich the readers on their path to progress, self-appraisal, and response. It is my hope that readers will approach these reflections from this perspective.

A Bundle of Joy

I HAD ALWAYS WANTED to spend a few moments with my reflections and to put down something before confronting the audience, but it seems that I could never achieve that feat while working in the parish. Anyway, I found this discipline again when I got the chance of a lifetime to work in the seminary in faraway Liberia. I consider it a wonderful occasion and the best experience I would ever have. So I cashed in on this experience to put together what I now see as a bundle of joy. This is not to say that these reflections were easy to come by. What is profound here is that I managed to accomplish a wish I had always kept in my thoughts. That is why it remains a bundle of joy for me and I hope also for those who would spend time with these reflections. I also hope that if one does find time to read this reflection, it will evoke those joyous moments I had when I shared this moving spiritual moment with the seminary community.

It is my hope also that those special moments in the communal efforts at prayer, which achieved pleasurable times, will bring blessings on those who make the effort to reflect on this work. My immediate community and audience was the student community of St. Paul's College Seminary in faraway Liberia. In this chapel, I celebrated Mass daily with the students and staff, and we shared the best part of our lives there. I hope that as I found those moments deeply rewarding, those who come across my bundle of joy find in it this wonderful experience.

My special thanks to the students and staff, who were very attentive, created the right environment, and made this time memorable. May God in His infinite mercy continue to bless us all.

—Rev. Donald Tyoapine Komboh, PhD
St. Paul's College Seminary, Gbarnga
Liberia, West Africa

Champions of Faith, Nobility, and Virtue[1]

To convert somebody go and take them by the hand and guide them.
St. Thomas Aquinas

C ONSIDER THIS, "SO in this way he died, leaving in his death an example of nobility and a memorial of courage, not only to the young but to the great body of his nation" (2 Maccabees 6:31). Dear brother priests and seminarians, it gives me great joy at the start of my teaching ministry to celebrate this Mass for you and with you. In the walls of the chapel of this noble institution, may I dedicate my little reflection to the Lord for the grace I have received since my arrival and the many favors I have continued to receive from both staff members and students. It is on this note that I want to join forces with the scripture and to point out that "Eleazar remained a man of nobility till death"(2 Maccabees 6:28); this is definitely a lesson that we can all learn—from him and the strong opinion that people had of him. Again, Zacchaeus was ready to give half his property to the poor, and if he had cheated anybody, he would pay him back four times the amount. Remember, fourfold restitution was required for one case only

---

[1] Being a reflection at Mass at the seminary chapel of St. Paul's College Seminary, Tuesday, Week 33, 2 Maccabees 6:18–31, Luke 19: 1–10, November 20, 2007.

as imposed by Jewish law, and Roman law demanded it of all convicted thieves. So Zacchaeus went further; he acknowledged the obligation in the case of any injustice for which he may have been responsible.

Notwithstanding his profession, no social ranks exclude salvation. "The son of man has come to seek out and save what was lost." Today, dear brothers, as priests and seminarians, we too can become champions of faith in our various capacities because we are considered people of nobility. Our situation was won for us through a special grace from God, and this makes us special. Let us preserve it with all our might and remain in our times the best examples we can be of the champions of our faith, nobility, and virtue in the various aspects we have been called to witness.

A Royal Choice and a Believer Decision

Preach the Gospel at all times. If necessary, use words.
St. Francis

OUR WORLD TODAY is characterized by choices and decisions to be made. Hardly a day passes without the challenge of making a decision being pushed upon us. We decide on who we are and what we want to be, and this is not easy at all. We make decisions as seminarians and formators about the expectations of society but most of all about God. So the quest for belonging and the hope of improvement continue unabated. Our first reading, therefore, presents to us the decision of a choice that is royal. Carefully chosen pupils with royal backgrounds were to serve as scribes, translators, scholars, archivists, and so on. Their lives were destined for the career of "letters." There is no doubt that the challenge was conscripted. The choice was precise and concise as well. The expectation of the king was that he would have people who would guide him on the delicate choice of administration and the running of so massive an empire. In earnest, he was preparing for better days in the future.

Among those chosen, the Hebrew boys led by Daniel were guided by beliefs. They wanted to hold on to their faith and tradition. No compromises would be made in the beliefs they held, and God was on their side. With a delicate meal of vegetables and faith, they turned out to be brilliant just the way the king wanted. I think, as believers, they took the path of faith and refused to compromise their beliefs regardless of the obvious discomfort it would bring to those around them. They were determined to make a difference and change their circumstances. These gentlemen won and remained for me models of our faith. As seminarians, we have to imbibe such winning ways to succeed in life. We know our background. Every day of our lives, these champions of faith should spur us to ask ourselves, "What decisions am I making for the Lord, and am I achieving them at all?"

The gospel is no different. Luke presents a scenario of those who make decisions and bring in gifts from the abundance of what they have. The rich give plenty maybe because they are blessed in their abundance. The poor may be tempted to say they don't have anything to give. But Jesus teaches this morning that the poor too from their poverty can give in all that they have. This widow becomes for us the champion of the believer's decision. If you have a problem with choices—I believe we all do—here is a teaching you can rely on. Let us give back to God all that we have and think we can live on, and we will see the miracles and transformations that will bring to our lives. It may be your schedule; it could be your studies, an illness, or a challenge—no matter the difficulty, let's give God all we have to live on, and he will surely transform us into something beautiful and challenging. If he did it for Daniel and his companions and made the widow go home a winner, surely he will make us seminarians and priests even better than what we can imagine. This is my prayerful wish for you this morning.[2]

---

[2] Being a reflection at Mass in the seminary chapel of St. Paul's College Seminary, Gbarnga, Monday, Week 34, Daniel 1:1–6, 8–20; Luke 21:1–4, November 26, 2007.

Produce Good Fruits or Be Thrown into the Fire
Matthew 3:10

Teach us to give and not count the cost.
St. Ignatius de Loyola

FOR A START, we celebrate the second Sunday of Advent, and it is with great joy that I welcome you to this celebration. I have had the rare privilege of being in this lovely country for the last month and have met with a few groups already. My association with these groups of seminarians, catechists, and laity shows the great promise the church in Liberia has, and I am proud to be part of these great promises. I want to believe that I will put in my best to develop the future of the church in this part of the world. On arrival, I was made welcome despite the recent history of our beloved country—a country that is so blessed yet has suffered so badly. My dear brothers, I see this as a privileged moment given to us. Those of us being formed now must resolve never to allow what happened before to repeat itself. As Christians and priests in the making, let us use all that is at our disposal to equip ourselves for the mission that the Lord is calling us to. Ours is a beautiful country, with lovely people and an elegant and vibrant society; let us take pride in this land and make it the best place to be.

DONALD TYOAPINE KOMBOH, PHD

A Call to Repentance

The readings this morning call us to rethink our nature. Because of the fallen nature of man, our ties with the Lord are broken. Man's fallen nature introduces sin to the world. This spells doom and disasters. Our lives, which were fully ordered by the Lord and his laws, are now under the spell of darkness and gloom. This fallen nature is so obstructive that even the animal kingdom is affected. This means that humanity has been completely polluted and all of nature, including the animals and plants, needs to be cleansed. The picture the prophet paints this morning is no different from what we have experienced in this country. In fact, if I am to describe it, I would say the sins of our fallen nature, despite the vivid depiction of the scriptures, is like "The 29th of October, 1985, when Doe was credited with 50.9% in the four way race to the presidency, 'commentators reacted' that the gloom that descended on Liberia that day was compared to the national gloom and stupefaction that enveloped the US the day President Kennedy was assassinated."[3] Dear brothers, once we give in to temptation and fall, the destructive effects snowball. There are obvious calamities, common sense and reason are thrown off, and the reign of evil often produces a ripple effect. But we have it from the gospel reading, a proclamation of a man called John the Baptist, who admonishes and calls for a change. His background is divine and miraculous. His lifestyle is austere and even bizarre, but his message and teachings are thought-provoking, penetrating, and troubling, but ultimately life-saving. He calls for repentance, a change of heart, a renunciation of sins. Once sin is renounced, the change of heart is in place. If we allow sin, then we dare God, and he backs off. Although he is ever ready to welcome any sinner who repents, we, for our part, must make the necessary effort.

---

[3] Paul Gilford, ed., New Dimension in African Christianity (Ibadan: Safer Books, 1993), 44.

Production of Fruits

How true is it and more so for this season, dear brothers, when we are preparing and making space for God, we become fruits that are bad. The Lord (the farmer) sows in tears, but reaps with joy. Our efforts also should be to sow in tears and reap with joy at harvest time. To sow in tears means to produce good fruits at the end. It is tasking and time-consuming. It is gradual and steady, but it is sure. Your time here is like that, my brothers; let's aim for the good fruits. It means we must work on ourselves; we must equip ourselves in a lot of ways. It is an intensive formation of life, a big challenge for those preparing to serve the Lord in these troubling times. The people we are facing are traumatized from years that knew violence without peace. We have a duty to bring this peace the gospels allude to, so we need to prepare. We need to avoid sin with a passion and provide a path and standard for our people. To produce good fruit, remember, means a lot of patience. We need to give in all we have to avail ourselves of the right formation in all facets of the formation being provided, be they spiritual, moral, academic, or otherwise.

Caught in the Fire

We must avoid the temptation of being caught in the fire. Out there is a lot frenzy and temptation. It seems a lot of opportunities are opened for you. Society knows you have a good education and a sound training and most of all, you are young, brilliant, and handsome. Its baits are numerous. You need to be holy to avoid sin, or you will be caught in the fire and be burnt. God forbid anyone is caught. Advent gives us this opportunity to prepare, spiritually and otherwise. Let us utilize this time and really prepare, just as the second reading concludes, "May the God of steadfastness and encouragement grant you to live in harmony with one another, in accordance with Christ Jesus, so that together you may with one voice glorify the God and Father of our Lord Jesus Christ" (Romans 15:5–6). This is my prayer wish for you this Sunday.[4]

---

[4] Being a Sunday homily at Mass in St. Paul's College Seminary, second Sunday of Advent (A), Isaiah 11:1–10, Romans 15:4–9, Matthew 3:1–12, December 9, 2007.

Toward a New Direction: Jesus's Love

If you are what you should be, you will set the whole world ablaze!
St. Catherine of Sienna

DEAR BROTHER PRIESTS and my admirable seminarians, it seems the love of God is gaining ground out there, from the proliferation of churches and expansive celebrations of religious festivities, especially such as the season we are just coming out from. One can quickly conclude that God's love predominates. Similarly, the period suggests that we love our neighbor from the way these celebrations were carried out. But St. John reiterates this morning that in loving God, we must keep his commandment, and it is only in keeping his commandments that we can actually say we love God. These commandments, he goes on to say, are "not difficult" because anyone who has been begotten by God has already overcome the world. This is our faith. But a quick retrospection from us will show that we should ask, in the course of these celebrations, did we really keep God's commandment? Some of us were actively involved in the celebrations. We were part of the "wining and dining," part of the endless socialization, and only God knows where the lines were drawn between a celebration of love and sin.

Others were passive in these celebrations, but the images and imaginings of the period are still running wild and are vivid in the minds of many people. However, we have the assurance of St. John this morning that if we are begotten by God, then he has already overcome the world. Let me carefully posit that all of us know God and are begotten by God, so whether we were active or passive about the recent happenings, let us fear not! God has already overcome the world. Dear brothers, this overcoming of the world is shown in a new direction: Jesus's love! St. Luke furnishes us with a picture. On entering the synagogue on a Sabbath day and having read from the scroll of the prophet Isaiah as it was written, Jesus said, "The Spirit of the Lord is upon me, because he has anointed me to bring good news to the poor. He has sent me to proclaim release to the captives and recovery of sight to the blind, to let the oppressed go free, to proclaim the year of the Lord's favor" (Luke 4:18–19). Jesus won the approval of all, when he proclaimed that the text was being fulfilled even as they listened—a new direction in the way of thinking, how to break new ground, the possibility of opening new avenues for the realization of God's love and plunging further afield into the inexhaustible mysteries of God. Jesus's love and way are inclusive of all the poor, lonely, and dejected. We all will find a place in his love. For those of us who are locked up or bottled up in various emotional strains, a new way is revealed. Jesus's love props up those who think they are downtrodden in society. In our community, all of us are inclusive of this love. In Jesus, God indeed has overcome the world. At the start of this year, brothers, let us be ever determined to love God and to keep his commandments. This new way and direction is only too clearly shown in Jesus's love. As seminarians and priests, this is our way and this is our faith.[5]

---

[5] Being a reflection at Mass in St. Paul College Seminary, Gbarnga, Christmas season, Thursday after Epiphany or January 10, 1 John 4:19–5:4, Luke 4:14–22, January 10, 2008.

Following Jesus without Counting the Cost

We always find that those who walked closest to Christ
were those who had to bear the greatest trials.
St. Teresa of Avila

A LOT OF THE time, we spend our lifetime chasing after molds and ideals created and sustained by society. At certain periods in the development of our lives, society expects certain behaviors from us as children, young adults, mature men and women, the elderly, and finally when we return to God and are committed to Mother Earth. We notice this gradual social stratification as we pick up these ideals and values and respond to these expectations in our growth process. As a girl, one is expected to marry at the age of marriage. After marriage, it is believed or expected once more that a child is the necessary result of this happy union (i.e., heterosexual marriage). But when, after a while, a child or children don't appear from the long overdue period, questions begin to emerge, and the parties involved in this marriage are put under pressure. More so, the wife or woman is put on edge. If the husband is not focused, it could be the beginning of an intense period in the lives of the couple. This is because society and its expectations affect and continue to challenge, thereby putting or creating a lot of strain in our lives.

This is the situation Hannah finds herself in this morning. She is taunted by her rival because she has no children. She is considered barren by the Lord in a society where to be barren connotes all kinds of inhibitions and worst of all sin. One feels with Hannah and can summarily relate to her experience. As seminarians and priests, we face a similar situation where we are expected to fit into a particular mold or ideal. We are expected to relate based on this prescribed mold, and woe betide you when you are found failing. The flag goes up, and society is quick to raise an alarm. In the end, we are either cast aside or labeled for life. The anguish of Hannah this morning corresponds to the lives that we live as people at the command of formation and those being formed.

However, we do know that in the process of socialization and development, there is always a light at the end of the tunnel. We have to stamp our feet and make our marks regardless of the burdens of society and the expectations of life. In this light, Jesus calls us this morning to repentance but more so to "follow" him. He wants to make us "fishers of men." He called the disciples by name, and they followed him, leaving everything behind. God calls each one by name. Everyone's name is sacred. The name is the icon of the person. It demands respect as a sign of the dignity of the one who bears it.[6] We are all called as individuals; we are known, identified, guided, and made to respond to this call of Jesus. In the midst of this complex, compelling, competing, and demanding world, Jesus fishes for men who will follow him and seek the hearts of others. This is a choice that can lead to estrangement, isolation, and even outright persecution. For those wanting to follow Jesus, no cost is counted. Everything is left behind, and Jesus is the ultimate. We too have made these choices. Some of us are in the process. Together, we are expected to leave everything and follow Jesus. It means no form of social estrangement or association nor any demand of society should stop us from following Jesus.

In following Jesus, we have to give him our all without counting the cost. We might have inhibitions. Let us bring them forward, and

---

[6] Catechism of the Catholic Church, 507.

he will heal us. For as the psalmist notes, "The Lord has been mindful of us; he will bless us; he will bless the house of Israel; he will bless the house of Aaron" (Psalm 115:12ff).[7]

---

[7] Being a reflection at Mass at St. Paul's College Seminary, Gbarnga, first week in ordinary time, year 11 (A), 1 Samuel 1:1–8, Mark 1:14–20, January 14, 2008.

St. Paul's Panegyric

Late have I loved you, O Beauty ever ancient,
ever new, late have I loved you!
St. Augustine

I N MODERN ETHICAL thought, "person" and "personality" play particularly important roles. The human personality implies three things: autonomy, self-achievement, and responsibility. Autonomy is to be in and of itself intrinsically self-sufficient. Self-achievement means what one as a person must achieve oneself by one's free, human actions. And responsibility is being able to give an account of oneself. All these become the foundation of all moral actions. Be that as it may, we notice from our readings, especially the first reading, the interplay of this action unfold in what seems to be a "panegyric of St. Paul's." In it, he is able to render an account of the new faith he now carries, how it all started, the various actors involved, and so on. Whether it satisfied his listeners is another issue entirely, but what is certain is that here is a "villain" who has turned into a "victor." In making this all-important choice, we read the hand of God at play at each decisive moment of his life.

His personality is dressed or robed anew. Life for him takes on a new meaning, opening up new dimensions and setting him apart for the start of an expansive missionary endeavor that was to surpass anything ever told of in his day. Although St. Paul tells us of his conversion, dear brothers, I see here an exciting new possibility from which we all can learn something. He is not afraid to tell of his past. His testimony is given in total conviction with all honesty and passion. His concern is not about exact details; needless to say, he is not bothered by exaggerations. He just recounts the story of his life with a childlike simplicity, an incredible transparency. His conviction is sure and absolute. "Jesus whom he was persecuting,"(Acts. 9:5) has healed him.

What then is the story of our life? Can it be recaptured with such an amazing slant of honesty, or is it to an extent so messed up that we would want to patch it before someone tells our story for us? Come to think of it, we probably have never seen a need to roll back on our lives' stories, let alone spare a thought for the development of our faith. We simply tag along and hope that our burning zeal for God will not run out of steam. But remember, Jesus has a mission for us, just like Paul. He showed himself to the eleven to proclaim the goodness to all creation. One who believes and is baptized will be saved. Anyone not baptized lacks the qualification to enter heaven, likewise those without belief in him. But he guarantees security. In his name, we will cast out devils, and we will have the gift of tongues. Snakes and poison will have no effect on us; however, we will lay hands on the sick, and they will recover. All these and more are possible only if we believe in him.

May our personality and life, like St. Paul's, be able to win souls for our Lord, and may people be able to read and identify with this all-important mission entrusted to us. Surely we can begin to redirect our lives to this purpose and be able to live the challenge our Lord calls us too. This for me is the reason why we are here, and this is my wish for us on this day when we celebrate the feast of the conversion of St. Paul.[8]

---

[8] Being a homily at Mass in the seminary chapel of St. Paul's College Seminary, Gbarnga, Bong County, the Feast of the Conversion of St. Paul, second week, Acts 22:3–16 or Acts 9:1–22, Mark 16:15–18, January 25, 2008.

The Virtuous, but Sinners to Repentance Luke 5:32

Pray as though everything depended on God. Work
as though everything depended on you.
St. Augustine

DEAR BROTHERS, THIS period in our liturgical calendar is characterized by a vocal and pleasant call for repentance in all fronts of our spiritual lives. At the moment, the church looks forward to all her children heeding this significant call. We all begin a very important period that will take us to the crowning of our cherished Christian traditions. Let us avail ourselves of this period and be able to stand for God in all that we do. The act of living itself is tasking, but living together is even more challenging. While tension and difficulties rear their ugly faces to the fore, peace and joy decide every so often to recede their calm presences to the backyards of our dormitories, hostels, and rectories. However, a careful look at our different situations and opportunities and diverse natures or even backgrounds suggests that indeed as sinners, we can truly ask the Lord, "Teach me your way, O Lord, that I may walk in your truth; give me an undivided heart to revere your name" (Psalm 86:11). This walking in his truth is recaptured again in the first reading from the prophet Isaiah, where he suggests, "The Lord will guide you continually, and satisfy your needs in parched places, and make your bones strong; and you shall be like a watered garden, like a spring of water, whose waters never fail" (Isaiah 58:11–12).

As priests and seminarians, we are called at this period of fasting, prayer, and repentances. Indeed, a clarion call has been made of us; it will demand a bit on our already crowded schedule, but this added feat to our schedule is the challenge of living a Christian life. We live in a sick world in need of healing. This healing will only come when in justice we are able to face this world in prayer and repentance. How many times have you been told you are useless, a sinner, a spare part in the wheel of progress, and because of you every other thing has gone wrong? Indeed, how many times have you felt yourself really a misfit in the midst of everything else right? Dear brothers, we indeed live in a sick society in need of our light, knowledge, and peace. While we take on this fasting with all our might by responding to justice in solidarity to the right cause, putting aside our prejudices and truly seeking the face of God, Jesus indeed can respond to those who think they are more virtuous, who prefer to hide under the banners of pharisaic spirituality, with "I have come to call not the righteous but sinners to repentance."(Luke 5:32)[9]

---

[9] Being a homily at Mass in St. Paul's College Seminary Chapel, Gbarnga, Bong County, Liberia, Saturday after Ash Wednesday, Isaiah 58:9–4, Luke 5:27–32, February 9, 2008.

The Will of the One Who Has Sent Us ... John 4:34

"Eat my flesh," [Jesus] says, "and drink my blood."
The Lord supplies us with these intimate nutrients, he
delivers over his flesh and pours out his blood, and
nothing is lacking for the growth of his children.
St. Clement of Alexandria

AS WE CELEBRATE today, the third Sunday of Lent, it is evident that the Lenten season is gradually moving to its climax, and we all are certainly participating in this prolonged retreat with all the desired intensity and strength. We thank the Lord for continuously guiding us and providing for all our needs, and it is our sincere desire once more that we will continue to aspire to his holiness with faith and courage. There exists a fundamental truth, which is that in moments of crisis, our abilities as capable leaders, opinionated persons, and respectable personalities are severely challenged; however, it is in these moments that we are expected to make responsible judgments for ourselves and for the Lord, whose mission we are effectively carrying out. This is more so as we are priests in the making and priests already called to this humble mission. The real challenge, therefore, my brothers this morning is to know the will of God and to obey the Lord's will in the most trying of circumstances and places.

There is no environment that presents such a challenge like the one of living together, pursuing a goal and hoping to arrive at a point together, as we happen to be doing here in this seminary compound. In the midst of worldly struggles, we hope that the time spent here in prayer, study, and development will help us to really discern the Lord's will for us and for the mission he has called us to. This discernment, dear brothers, takes time; it is conjured up in personalities, temperaments, social and emotional conditions, and even physical attributes. All of these are and will be part of the will to be discerned in knowing ourselves as we hope to know God's own will. The interesting thing is that our Lord is patient, and through this heavenly virtue, he is able to teach us. As ardent students, we hope to follow.

We notice this attribute in the first reading of today. The people of Israel, we are told in the book of Exodus, were tormented by thirst. A disaster had emerged, their most trying time had come, and what sort of reaction were they going to put forward to the Lord? Their first reaction was to confront the prophet of the Lord, Moses. He had to have ready answers because it was a situation of life and death, a situation of trial (Massah) and confrontation (Meribah). Here, it is the Lord who is being confronted and put to the test. For his part, the Lord answered and solved the situation in his patience and guidance. Victory was won for the Lord. An imminent disaster was averted, and the episode became a lesson for life for us all to see as witnesses to the truth.

A repeated case is showcased in the gospel reading of how our Lord Jesus insists that his food is to do "the will of God." His love and accomplishment is to ensure that the truth is told, and salvation is won for all, whether Jew or Gentile. Saints or sinners, we are all to come to the knowledge of the truth. We all will come to this knowledge of the truth not by the strength of someone's powerful preaching, although this could be one such way, not by someone's power of persuasion—to be honest, that too has its own advantage—and not by enforcing rules and regulations, which to my mind also contribute positively to one's development and career. It is by coming to terms with oneself in the knowledge of Christ by yourself, having seen, heard, and known about this Jesus who is passionate about the will of the Father. We can say with the Samaritans to the woman that "it is no longer because of what you said that we believe, for we have heard for ourselves, and we know that this is truly the Savior of the world" (John 4:42).

Let me say this for a fact; it is true that the will of the father is not a thing that can be easily discerned, but we have the lessons from our Lord. He alone is the source of everlasting waters, the living water. Whoever drinks this water of his will never go thirsty again. But "those who drink of the water that I will give them will never be thirsty. The water that I will give will become in them a spring of water gushing up to eternal life" (John 4:14). Dear brothers, how else can I explain the will of the Lord for us; my educated guess is that we conform to what the Lord has admonished us to do. We are to strive to drink from the well of the Lord. How beneficial a Lenten gift this is. The strength of our prayers and reflection, repentance, and penance are parceled up in this most perfect gift if we are able to drink from the living waters that the Lord provides.

One can say today that this seemed to be the most fundamental lack that we all have; we live and believe that from our own well, we can draw the waters that we have stored there to survive. It doesn't surprise me, therefore, when in crisis moments, we revert to our inner self, hoping that the strength of our inner resources will be able to cope with this situation. But the truth is the well soon runs dry because we have failed to drink and draw from the Lord's well. Life in its many forms and teachings has taught me that when we stay with the Lord and present our feebleness to him, he will teach us the ways to confront and overcome the most pressing of needs and problems. It might be a personality clash, an economic interest, low self-esteem, executive stress, spiritual paralysis, maladjusted personalities, family squabbles, or parental loss—the list is endless. What I propose is simple. The Lord himself is already aware of the difficulties and the challenges. All that he asks of us is to be able to discern his will and drink from his stream so that the waters that flow from him become a spring of eternal life.

In this third Sunday of Lent, when we discover that our "well still runs dry," we are reassured with St. Paul that "God proves his love for us in that while we still were sinners Christ died for us" (Romans 5:8).

The intention is not to remain in sin but to save us from our sins. As we continue our Lenten observances, we have to rise above our sins. This is a big challenge that confronts us but is not beyond us. As a student, I must make pertinent efforts to ensure that my prayer life is renewed, my spirituality is focused, my intellectual life is integrated, and, above all, my person is tailored toward the right directions. The same goes for an individual who seeks the path of justice in his or her chosen career as a teacher, an economist, a minister, or a senator, not forgetting us, the priests, as well. We all have to join our Lord in doing the will of the one who sent him. This is our mission and mandate. We cannot afford to fail, especially now that we have all the assurance from the Lord. The psalmist concludes even better when he declares, "Do not harden your hearts, as at Meribah, as on the day at Massah in the wilderness" (Psalm 95:8). [10]

---

[10] Being a homily as Mass in St. Paul's College Seminary, Gbarnga, Bong County, Liberia, third Sunday of Lent (A), Exodus 17:3–7; Romans 5:1–2, 5–8; John 4:5–42, February 24, 2008.

Trapped[11]

We will either accuse ourselves or excuse ourselves.
St. John Vianney

WE LIVE IN a world today that glamorizes sexual appeal. It has found its way into all that we do. Watch commercials on television for soap, cosmetics, or any product whatsoever; if the ad does not portray a naked woman either partially or completely, the company may not make great sales. What makes great sales today must be advertised by a supermodel in the weirdest of dresses or sunglasses or the most erotic of postures. Take it or leave it, this is what is marketable and selling. The same goes for books and magazines and a host of other periodicals. This is the world today, and we have found ourselves in this great mess. I guess it is enjoyed by a great majority because nothing suggests that it will go away for a long time to come. It is not surprising when this desire is not checked. It would be completely wrong if you shifted the blame onto someone other than yourself. I have often felt that the constant defaming of one's personality is a new form of psychology that has continued to sell on the wrong side of the planet in the name of "my body," "my own," and the "me" consciousness theories.

---

[11] Being a homily at Mass at the seminary chapel of St. Paul's College Seminary, Gbarnga, Liberia, Monday, fifth week of Lent, Daniel 13:1–9, 15–17, 19–30, 33–62; John 8:1–11, March 10, 2008.

When you think of it, at face value, you may restrict this kind of desire to a particular age, but it seems from the foregoing that the sexual urge, as we have read from the first reading, defiles age and continues to stick its head out in even the ugliest of situations and circumstances. Does one blame the elders in our rabbinic story this morning who wanted to get a shot at their sexual exploits from one of their very own? Their contrived plot was well designed. Their initial shot hit the target. The only problem was that the victim chose another option. "I choose not to do it; I will fall into your hands, rather than sin in the sight of the Lord" (Daniel 13:23). However, the elders were not done yet; their machination was masterminded by the desire and perpetration of darkness, their intent was malicious, and the outcome of their exploit was either victory or death. These elders were, to use a familiar slang or term of my rector, on top of things. But as the story turns out, the reverse is the case. With the introduction of a new entrant, Daniel, the story becomes replete with lessons. At least one case shows that fidelity to God, especially to his will and law, will definitely lead to winning God's glory and eventual happiness. The Lord is indeed the avenger of the innocent. This theme echoes itself in the episode of Jesus and the woman caught in adultery. Again, the elders are quick to lay blame on the shoulders—or should I say the lap, maybe specifically the bottom of the woman—and they demand an answer from Jesus. You all know that our Lord condemned the sin, not the sinners, and the reactions of those same perpetrators of evil cast a slur on their behaviors. So they had to leave, beginning with the eldest. It shows that in both cases of our first reading and the gospel, our sisters in the story are trapped. This reveals the constant position of women in society. They either agree to this seemingly maligning situation, or they are stuck in this tragedy forever. However, the elders have failed and brought condemnation on themselves. While we condemn the elders this morning for this woeful display of passion at an age when we feel they should be torchbearers because of their years and the most profitable of all longevity, I beg to show that it will seem these sexual urges and appetites defile age and wisdom. We too are already elders because the Greek word used is presbyter, meaning "elder," suggesting that those of us who are already elders in the church and who aspire to be elders have a lesson to learn. As for our Lord Jesus, it was because he did things like this that they believed he deserved to die.

As this critical time of Lent, we need to check and reexamine our desires and appetites for everything—be it food in the physical and spiritual senses, our attitudes and inclinations, or our wants and desires, not to forget our needs and perspectives. The list of longings can go on, but these have their consequences. Our Lord shows us this morning that in all, it is the sin that must be condemned, not the sinner. However, in his case, it was both the sinner and the sin that the Jews held in contempt, and they destroyed him. Although trapped, he chose to die preferring innocence than to go against the will of "the one who sent him,"(John7:16). May I just say that as priests and seminarians, there will be times when we will have to do likewise as an example of the love we have for God for the multitude of followers. This period of Lent calls for that more so as we come to the close of it all. May we learn to go a step further. The Lord himself will see us through.

And Light of the Nations ... Isaiah 42:6b

All the darkness in the world cannot extinguish
the light of a single candle.
St. Francis

WE BEGIN THIS wonderful day with the understanding that we are at the threshold of our church's calendar. It is the beginning of the week of our faith. We are indeed grateful for this opportunity to once again have the pleasure of reflecting on our journey to eternity. For the last four weeks, we have been involved in a journey of faith together, in fasting and prayer, and involved in corporal and spiritual works of mercy. Some of us are deeply enmeshed in strict devotional practices that are characteristic of this time. As we proceed to this final leap of faith, we are once again introduced to the beauty of the scriptures and what to expect from the prophet Isaiah.

However, let me quickly say that it is a fact of life that we go through life almost uncertain of what to expect at each given time. We may have all the information on a given subject, the necessary technical advances and advisers on hand should we delve into areas of perceived danger and need. There are ready experts who are only too willing to throw their weight on our behalf so that an imminent danger is averted. Despite these precautionary measures that modern man has placed for himself regarding life's most threatening circumstances, we don't seem to come out clean in these matters. The wrong decisions seem to be the ones on the ground. The worst mistakes are made, and life is ruined from all sides by the pains of betrayal, penury, religious bigotry, denial, and, worst of all, outright wars, miseries, and destructions. There seems to be only darkness around us and no light is envisioned. That is why I agree with the portrait of Isaiah—light of the nations—which will be a recurring theme in this holy week.

Permit me, therefore, brothers and sisters, to focus my mind a little on this most noble metaphor of light in the scriptures. At the story of the incarnation, we read beautifully too that "there will be no gloom for those who were in anguish. In the former time he brought into contempt the land of Zebulon and the land of Naphtali, but in the latter time he will make glorious the way of the sea, the land beyond the Jordan, Galilee of the nations" (Isaiah 9:1). This light is about to be illumined in the activities that will take place these few days to wrap up all that the Lenten season has enjoined us to do. Our parents were prepared for this light in the midst of their pains, worries, and lives lived with threats of destruction and death. So, a light had shone to open them up to the radiances of God's glory. So it is with us who piously and promptly conducted ourselves properly in the sight of God these few days.

Indeed, our lives and conduct would have spelled doom and destruction for us, but it is a thing of joy to know that in Jesus we are glorified, for the time of his glorification has come. The chief architects of evil in this world will continue to plot, plan, and try to execute their projects of ills and destructions, but the light of Christ will continue to radiate in the hearts of his many followers. This light will illumine our thoughts and actions and will enable us to achieve the highest pedestal of our dreams, as long as we are glorified in him. Let us pray this morning for the grace to go through the remaining ceremonies of this week with a sincere and devoted heart, and the good Lord will see us through with joy.[12]

---

[12] Being a homily at Mass in the chapel of St. Paul's College Seminary, Gbarnga, Liberia, Monday, Holy Week, Isaiah 42:1–7, John 12:1–11, March 17, 2008.

The Bread of Life ...

Give something, however small, to the one in need.
For it is not small to one who has nothing. Neither is
it small to God, if we have given what we could.
St. Gregory Nazianzen

WE HAVE IT from our Christian theology that the blood of the martyrs is indeed the seed of the church.[13] What we have witnessed this morning is the humble beginnings of the early church; this is a natural conclusion of the narrative that we have followed for the last two days. It is also the beginning of Saul's campaign against the Christians, and it will lead to the sequel of Paul's conversion. Interestingly too it is a note on the church persecuted and scattered, which serves as an important introduction to Philip's mission. Against this background then, it is quite revealing to say it is the humble beginning of not only the church but everything one puts his or her hands on in life. Does it surprise you, my brothers, that when you embark on a journey to the unknown, like we are doing now, trying in all facets to discern our vocations and callings as priests to be, that the anticipated anxieties about what awaits you as you travel not only creates panic but always puts you on a challenge daily? The early disciples are on the run

---

[13] Kathryn Greene-McCreight, "United in Suffering: Martyrdom as Christian Vocation," The Christian Century, September 17, 2015, https://www.christiancentury.org/article/2015-09/united-suffering.

this morning for fear of persecution, and these were the prophecies already foretold by our Lord himself. He warned that they were going to be dragged before governors and rulers on account of his name, but they were not to fear; he would be with them to the end of time.

The truth is that we must always remember that as Christians in the world, we are expected to continue to show that we are really prepared for all these eventualities. We too have met with situations where it seems all hope is gone, and the race we embark on seems so futile. The challenge exists in society today where we have to give hope and courage to a world that seems restive with anxieties. To barely live another day is a record, a struggle for all kinds of things, from shelter, food, and work to a reason to be alive. I am told that the situation is better, but how much better can this situation be when around us we bitterly face abject poverty, low levels of education that is hardly affordable, and an intense and acute shortage of the basic necessities of life, like drinking water, good hospitals, and passable roads, not to mention electricity and the like?

Brothers, the gospel tells us this morning to believe, that our Lord is the bread of life and he who believes in him shall never hunger and never thirst. I do believe in him, and it is the basis for all my life and mission work. As priests and seminarians, we have a mandate from these beliefs of ours to continue to give and preach these words of God. The resurrection experience and the faith of the early disciples are clear testimonies and manifestations of these beliefs. We not only may show that we believe in our works, but we will try to radiate that belief in our lives. Every new day should make us come to the belief that we are disciples of our Lord in a restless world of passions and sorrows and only "I Am" is the solution to our problems.

We pray in this Mass, therefore, that "I Am" will continue to rain down his blessings on those of us who believe and continue to carry out these demanding tasks of his despite the persecution and strife that seem to follow, for heaven indeed is our goal and the Lord himself is our final abode.[14]

---

[14] Being a homily delivered at Mass in the seminary chapel of St. Paul's College Seminary, Gbarnga, Liberia, Wednesday, third week of Easter, Acts 8:1–8; John 6:35–40, April 9, 2008.

My Areopagus Experience

Our hearts were made for You, O Lord, and
they are restless until they rest in you.
St. Augustine of Hippo

IT SHOULD NOT come as a surprise when we hear people talk
about their experiences and the way the Lord has touched them in
life, the fate that awaits them often after a traumatic experience,
or, as we heard the preacher put it yesterday, an expression of the faith
that we have in something. To a large extent, we are the product of our
making in the way we tell our stories and the passion that they evoke in
our listeners. The speech that St. Paul delivered today is born out of the
experience he had and treasured. The confidence he puts in the Lord
to share it with those who cared to listen is monumental. His listeners
may have been people of distinction and substance, who would have
prided themselves on having reached a privileged stature in learning
and education. But the truth remains that it is never too late to learn,
particularly when it comes to the things of the Lord himself. He was
lucky to have been listened to and to have had some who willingly
became believers.

This seems to be the lot of those of us who will become preachers
of the gospels, custodians of our cherished traditions, and better still,
keepers of the treasures of faith. We will have to live daily with the
experience of those who may want to listen to us but due to cowardice

and the pressure of this world may choose to decline. My position is simple—we try to do all we can to experience the power of truth, which the resurrection experience shares with us. We are told this morning in the gospel that the Lord himself said, "When the Spirit of truth comes, he will guide you into all the truth; for he will not speak on his own, but will speak whatever he hears, and he will declare to you the things that are to come,"[15] meaning there are times when we may just have to wait for the spirit to show us the way and the right thing to do. We must discern the spirit to know the right thing, be it in the prayers we say, the activities that we do in the seminary, the confessions we treasure, or the hidden patches of space that are buried in the recesses of our life. Knowing when to approach the spirit of truth is the ultimate.

St. Paul had an areopagus experience and spoke in a manner that he converted a few to the Lord. It is my prayer this morning that we seek for the spirit that is promised us, which will lead us to the complete truth. We may have a lot of fears and worries and may sometimes be confused and traumatized by a particular anxiety or tormented by a thought that is not going and remains in the same venue, making us feel guilty. I propose that we wait on the Lord and ask him for all the love and protection. As the psalmist says this morning, "Let them praise the name of the Lord, for his name alone is exalted; his glory is above earth and heaven."[16] Let us pray, for all that we will do may be taken from the Lord. And may the spirit of the risen Lord lead us to the complete truth. [17]

---

[15] John 16:13, New Revised Standard Version Bible, Catholic Edition (copyright 1989, 1993).

[16] Psalm 148:13, New Revised Standard Version Bible, Catholic Edition (copyright 1989, 1993).

[17] Being a homily delivered at Mass in the seminary chapel of St. Paul's College Seminary, Gbarnga, Bong County, Liberia, Wednesday, sixth Sunday of Easter, Acts 17:15, 22–18:1; John 16:12–15, April 30, 2008.

The Hour Has Come ... John 17:1

You cannot be half a saint; you must be a
whole saint or no saint at all.
St. Therese of Lisieux

THERE IS A popular African adage that is rendered in many forms depending on one's usage. My variant of it reads thus: What an elder sees sitting down, a child may climb the tallest mountain and not be able to see. This is the glaring picture that seems to be the atmosphere here in the seminary these remaining few weeks as we approach the end of the year. As elders and teachers, we are privileged and may see certain things that you, our dear students, may not see and understand. It is probably based on these pious sentiments that we exhort you on a daily basis. It is my desire also that one day, you may come to the complete knowledge of the truth, but before that happens, many of us may have to undergo testing. Gold is usually tested by fire. What is more is that the scriptures this morning also strengthen this picture. We see in both readings the visible expressions of Paul and Jesus who are about to leave behind their followers, and as we all know, it is not easy finding the right parting words.

St. Paul speaks this morning as a departing pastor and even hints at his death. He spent some time in advising the elders of mellitus in Asia to be vigilant and selfless and show tremendous charity to the flock that they would be shepherding. In this speech, he paints the portrait of a faithful apostle who has tended the flock and is now about to leave. In contrast, Jesus makes a prayer for himself and the apostles, showing in this prayer the oneness he has with his father and going further to proclaim his mission and highlight how this mission of his had clearly revealed his name and who he is. He has taught them the entire truth that he has learned from the father. The apostles in turn have come to appreciate and know the father—but the hour has come. He is going back to the father. What he expects is the vigilance, selflessness, and charity that the apostle Paul speaks of. This is what our Lord expects as he prepares to send us his spirit.

These cardinal virtues of vigilance, selflessness, and charity that are expected of the apostles are also the focal point of our formation. More so, as agents of evangelization in a highly sophisticated world, seminarians and priests may need to be vigilant because there are many who may want to steal the sheep that the Lord has entrusted to us. This entails a careful and well-coordinated life of prayer, openness, transparency, determination, and excellence. We cannot achieve this vigilance in an atmosphere of animosity and suspicion. In the very deep recesses of our hearts, we may have to be sincere with ourselves. However, the Holy Spirit, whom we are preparing to receive, dwells in the heart that is selfless and full of charity. This must be the rule that governs us. We must live in charity, and it should guide all our actions. I do believe that in love, we would be able to address all our needs and desires to the one we believe is not going to leave us orphans. As we come to the end of the year and we are expecting the spirit, the hour has come for us to be serious and prepare to receive this spirit with joy. I say all this to you because I am an elder myself.[18]

---

[18] Being a homily delivered at Mass at the seminary chapel of St. Paul's College Seminary, Gbarnga, Bong County, Liberia, Tuesday, seventh week of Easter, Acts 20:17–27, John 17:1–11, May 6, 2008.

Are You without Perception? Mark 8:21

When you encounter difficulties and contradictions, do not
try to break them, but bend them with gentleness and time.
St. Francis de Sales

ONE OF THE most fascinating things about today's first
reading is its practicality. We all know and are aware of the
basic facts of life and that as Christians we are trying to win
the crown of glory that the Lord has prepared for us. We look toward
heaven, and that seems to be our goal. We are loyal to this, and we strive
in various measures for that goal. At our various command posts and
observatories, we daily seek to chisel out a way, specifically to create
a path that will help us to arrive at that goal. There is no gain saying
then that when trials and tribulations come, we are adept at ensuring
that we are able to overcome these challenges. As seminarians, we are
subjects of truth, disciples of virtue, and hopefully champions of God's
graces. It means that for most of our lifetime, we will continue to meet
with trials and temptations! So, we must chide ourselves this morning
to remain faithful to the very end. May our time well spent here in the
seminary grounds prepare us for this challenge that hopefully will be
part of our lives, and may we leave here in such a way that there will
be no regrets when we are out of here.

As I reflect on James this morning, the words of the gospel are also edifying, especially the same practicality in language is underscored. The disciples are exhorted "to be open and to be on guard." This language of scripture does not betray words but hinges on the heart of the matter for the disciples. Although they were slow to understanding, this is an invitation on the part of our Lord to the disciples to forget their materialistic preoccupations and to reflect upon his mission, which he had highlighted in the miracles. If we focus on the Lord and his works, he will be the one to take care of our needs. There will be abundance for us and our measures will be pressed down, shaken, and filled to the brim. The difficulty we have as seminarians and priests is that we have been surrounded by a highly materialistic culture that has eaten into our systems. We are rated by what we have and our latest acquisitions, be it in our electronics or the sophistication of our cars. There are stepped competitions in various forms as to who has done what and has been where. The yeast that our Lord asks us to be on guard against today is fervently within our fold.

When you see young men clandestinely involved in a heated argument, tempers are flared up, and the discussion is almost devolving into a shouting match, make no mistake; just attempt an inquiry into that venture, and you will discover to your uttermost dismay that the debate was all about who owned the latest of these acquisitions we are talking of—electronics, computers, cars, and so on. None of us is exempt from this. We just have to check our yearnings and see how we can become aware of these materialistic tendencies that have crept into our ministry. We are to rely on the Lord, and he will show us the way to God. He has done this in his ministry. If we cannot see it, then the question addressed to his disciples this morning is only so apt. Are you without perception? We pray with the psalmist this morning when he notes in our responsorial psalms, "Happy the man to whom you teach, O Lord." [19]

---

[19] Being a homily delivered at Mass at the seminary chapel of St. Paul's College Seminary, Gbarnga, Bong County, Liberia, Tuesday, sixth week in ordinary time, James 1:12–18, Mark 8:14–23, May 13, 2008.

Winning the Hearts
of the People

The dress of the body should not discredit the good of the soul.
St. Cyprian

T HE READINGS THAT we hear from the Old Testament are a conclusion of the long battle of Elijah and the prophets of Baal on Mount Carmel. A decision had to be made. The battle line had been drawn, and the target was to win the hearts of the people of Israel back to God. Remember, these were people who had suffered because of their beliefs in foreign gods, which ultimately could not save them. In this process, they had incurred the wrath of God, which meant a period of drought that ushered in pains and persecution. With the victory, the king is asked to go back and to eat and drink for the rains have come. This is the victory that has been fought for and won with hard labor, requiring a victorious celebration. It came as a resolute decision that despite the uncertainties and adversities that befell the land of Israel, there still remained a true prophet of God to carry out his cause.

Similarly, our Lord invokes us to build virtues that are deeper than those of the Pharisees and Scribes, or else we will be barred from heaven. Brothers, permit me to reflect on this theme because this has remained a constant refrain in my thoughts. The Pharisees and Scribes, as we discover in the New Testament, were in constant battle with our Lord in his mission. As we see, our Lord challenged these groups of people. Should we not wonder at the fierce way in which our Lord confronted them and ask questions? Could it not be that more or less we ourselves are products of this kind of attitude and disposition? And there seemed to be a trademark of the Pharisees and Scribes that our Lord frequently challenged. When we run a check on who they are, we may find, among other things, that these men were experts of the law and committed to ensuring that not a letter of the law was contravened. As proud possessors of the laws and word of God, they ensured its promotion and enrichment. They were not just passive observers, but custodians and keepers of the rich traditions of the laws of God. They also invested time in seeing to it that the laws were kept and obeyed to the letter. In this process, they lost the spirit of the laws and became chained to literal interpretations, making them abstract and mere legalistic prescriptions. This spirit of the laws is what our Lord sought and fought for with the Pharisees and Scribes.

Little wonder that our Lord insists that "we must have learnt," but he says this: none of us is worthless in the sight of God, and we must get rid of our anger before we can bring our sacrifice to the altar of the Lord. We must make amends with those who offend us, and this should be done in good time. Maybe we can look at ourselves critically. A quick notice is that we are a little like the Pharisees in our dealings, good at observing the rules and keeping the traditions. Oh! Did I forget exerting the authority as given to us by virtue of ordination? How about the spirit behind the laws? Are we just interested in keeping these laws without taking into cognizance the actors involved in the laws? Are we humans or mere robots that we want to make into sacramental machines to churn out sacraments at the end of our stay in the seminary? If we are humans, then our virtue must be deeper so that we can win back the hearts of men. That goes for all of us priests and seminarians.[20]

---

[20] Being a homily delivered at Mass in the chapel of St. Paul's College Seminary, Gbarnga, Bong County, Liberia, Thursday, tenth week, 1 Kings 18:41–46, Matthew 5:20–26, June 12, 2008.

The Inheritance of
My Ancestors

The source of justice is not vengeance but charity.
Saint Bridget of Sweden

PROMINENT JEWISH RABBI Harold Kushner in one of his books, 'Who Needs God,' observes "our challenge in a mobile, individualistic, competitive society is to capture the closeness of the sect without its exclusivity." I think this spirit of the sect was what the king needed much more than resorting to the queen, who seemed to have another agenda. Indeed, Jezebel's shrewdness enabled her to get the vineyard for her husband, Ahab, but the method was cruel and cold. This was "the inheritance of his ancestor" snatched away from him because it was close to the king's court and a possession that the king wanted. This was done in total disregard of the existence and importance of the person of Naboth and what he represented. Does this not suggest the price one continually pays for being on the margin? But as it is echoed in our responsorial psalm today, "Give heed to my groaning, O Lord," seems to be the only tool available for the plight of the downtrodden. In the sect exists a spirit, and behind the spirit is the visible expression of a bountiful Lord and Savior who alone understands and cushions the pains and rejection of the poor.

A similar response is advised in the gospel, when our Lord responds to the disciples about what they were used to and what is now referred to in a new way. Offer no resistance! This reminds me of the proverbial story of some gentlemen involved in a shouting match that turned into a fight. In the instance, one gave a slap to the other fellow who happened to be a Christian, reminding him of this scriptural text. Admittedly, the lad gave him his other cheek. Instead, the gentleman man took a jab in his stomach. At this juncture, the Christian fellow pounced on the guy and gave him the beating of his life, stressing that the scriptural injunction specified the cheek, not the stomach. Indeed, this periscope does not forbid reasonable defense against unjust aggression, still less opposition to evil in the world. Allow me to emphasize our collective and social actions as seminarians in formation and as priests and the need to remember the social teachings of the church and the fundamental option for the poor. Justice issues are intrinsic issues for the church, and they form a constitutive element of her teaching. There will be no peace if there is no justice. Naboth's refusal to give away the inheritance of his ancestors earned him the supreme price for it. But we have to remember that the Lord demands that we give without counting the cost and without turning away anyone. This is a lesson that begins right here and includes all of us. In our respective situations, we are expected to give, and this is the expectation that must be reflected in the way we relate with one another and how we are involved in the lives and actions of all. My prayer at this time is that we will remember the cherished traditions of our ancestors and keep them.[21]

---

[21] Being a homily delivered at Mass in the chapel of St. Paul's College Seminary, Gbarnga, Bong County, Liberia, Monday, eleventh week, 1 Kings 21:1–16, Matthew 5:38–42, June 16, 2008.

Come to God with Boldness

God gives each one of us sufficient grace ever
to know His holy will and to do it fully.
St. Ignatius of Loyola

DEARLY BELOVED IN Christ, in this exceptional year, which the Holy Father has dedicated to the study, prayer, and activities of the apostle Paul. It is only fitting that at the start of an academic year like this, we earnestly pray and seek to enjoy the fruits of the exceptional life that the apostle lived and left for us as a lasting legacy for all times. As we begin this academic year, therefore, let us seek the wisdom of our elders, the counsel of the wise and learned, but above all, the direction of the spirit in all that we intend to achieve in this unfolding academic year. We hope to achieve this as we come to God with boldness, with the simplicity of a childlike affection that tends to glow with the excitement of a father proud of an obedient son.

Our readings this morning are very instructive. The apostle Paul, using very strong language, not only lashes on the Galatians for their lack of understanding but throws a lovely challenge on those of us who are hearers of the word this day. What we have is a reaction to something! While I do not want to get caught in the argument before now, a comment on how it is ending is quite edifying. The bone of contention had to do with faith and the law, a situation which even today does provoke a lot of interest in many quarters. However, the apostle

Paul reproves the Galatians for their folly in suffering themselves to be drawn away from their faith—and not only that but also from several considerations—to impress them with a sense of it. Similarly, he proves the doctrine of justification by faith without the work of the law. One thing is foremost, and this is that the consideration of the honors and privileges we have been admitted to as Christians should shame us out of the folly of apostasy and backsliding. He subsequently threw a challenge out for the Galatians for them to consider the miracles worked and whether they were the things of faith or the works of the law!

The gospel projects the idea of opportunity, fervency, and constancy in prayer. We must come to God with boldness and confidence for what we need, as a man goes to the house of his neighbor or friend whom he knows and who loves him and is inclined to be kind to him—a situation I have referred to elsewhere as praying to God with an attitude. Remember, we come to God for bread that is needed as something we cannot do without, for others and ourselves. Our desire to know God should propel us to come to him with boldness, as a channel not brought to us by our folly and carelessness. But it should be that providence has led us to it. This hopefully will be done in prayer and watchfulness in the same way with all the perseverance. The truth of the matter, dearly beloved in Christ, is that we should seek for the gift of the spirit. We all must do it earnestly and constantly pray for it, and the Lord will give us more. I am saying this particularly because of the ruggedness with which the apostle attacks the Galatians for their lack of faith. This is about the same principle our Lord uses in stepping us up in prayer. So as we face a new academic year, with a Pauline year for guidance, may the thoroughness with which the saint attached to his work be a launching pad for us in our dealings this year—be they in prayer and work, at play or study, and most of all in our development as future priests.[22]

---

[22] Being a homily delivered at St. Paul Seminary, Gbarnga, Bong County, Liberia, twenty-seventh week, Galatians 3:1–5, Luke 11:5–13, Thursday, October 8, 2008.

Purchased by a Higher Price

We are to love God for Himself, because of a twofold reason;
nothing is more reasonable, nothing more profitable.
St. Bernard of Clairvaux

DEARLY BELOVED IN Christ, at this moment of economic crisis and more so being a year specially dedicated to the activities marking the great celebrations of our most cherished and amiable apostle Paul, we cannot but help being thankful for such a wonderful reading this morning. The readings all evoke special spiritual sentiments; we are made to know that among many other things, we are blessed with spiritual gifts. Clearly, we are reminded that to those whom the Lord blesses, he adds spiritual gifts and heavenly things. For me, this is absolutely advantageous because not only have I a desire to possess these spiritual gifts in my life, and I long more for these heavenly gifts, but the thrust of this periscope is that God looks into the heart not at our external appearances. Here lies my strong conviction as the reading suggests that we as priests, as religious, and importantly as seminarians must always remember that it is the heart that the Lord is interested in, although we may most times claim that it is from the abundance of the heart that grace abounds. Let us remember that the heart matters a lot.

Permit me to say that we are purchased by a higher price, and this is the blood of Jesus. This is done through the riches of God's grace.

Redemption is through Christ. May we put our trust in God, never tiring despite our predicaments. I know that there are a lot of these difficulties, but it is necessary to go through this process so that the quality of our faith and love for God will be fully appreciated. We are indeed faced with all sorts of fears and challenges; however, as the prophets of old, whom the gospel comments on, had to face persecutions of all sorts in the name of our Lord to inherit these spiritual gifts and heavenly blessings, so may our inspiration be broadened by their faith. May the heart of each one of us be spurred by the commitments of our fathers in faith, their industry, their dedication, their piety, and supremely their sense of love. Most of all, fueled by the zeal of the gospel, it will be an enduring call to duty on our parts as priests. For our seminarians, may it continue to strengthen your resolves to acquire this most cherished price, which we all in our own capacities have longed for! Remember the psalmist this morning. The Lord has shown his salvation especially to those who want to possess it.[23]

---

[23] Being a homily delivered at Mass in the chapel of St. Paul College Seminary, Gbarnga, Bong County, Liberia, Thursday, twenty-eighth week, Ephesians 1:1–10, Luke 11:47–54.

A Great Deal
Given on Trust

Charity is the form, mover, mother, and root of all virtues.
St. Thomas Aquinas

DEAR BROTHERS, WE have it from scriptures this morning how Paul recounts his special appointments, which he indicates have been given to him by God's grace to preach the unsearchable riches of Christ. As a minister made by God's grace, he comes clean and notes that he was the least of the apostles; he doesn't think he can equate himself with any other, having persecuted the church and its disciples. He feels humbled to even be considered an apostle, and makes it clear that he is indeed the least of these apostles. But by a mighty treasure of mercy, grace, and love, he has this special revelation from Christ to carry on this mission. It would seem that we too can at least associate our call in some dramatic fashion with that of the apostle Paul, for we have been called in some way or the other. It is God who is calling us for himself, importantly, to be with him and for a specific mission, like the apostle will want us to know.

The gospel highlights most exceedingly a noble call for vigilance, since he calls us to himself for a mission; vigilance is for those who want to stay with Jesus. We do not know when the master will come, so we need to be alert to all our duties and must man these duty posts with the greatest diligence. With Peter and the other apostles, we are made stewards of God's household, to preach the gospel, administer the ordinance of Christ, and appeal to the seals of the covenant of grace. Our primary business is to give to God's children their portion of meat accordingly. As ministers, we must be both skillful and faithful. We must make ourselves servants to all. This portion of meat is clearly found in our public preaching and personal application, for all this is given to us on trust—a greater capacity of mind, more knowledge of learning, an appreciable acquaintance with sacred scriptures, and more, all are to be rendered accordingly. Happy those servants whom the Lord finds busy at their employments upon his arrival. He will reward them a great deal. As seminarians who aspire for a place at the Lord's employment, we are admonished this morning to strive for doing the Lord's will. At our disposal is the opportunity to muster all that our learning and environment provides to try to fathom the Lord's will correctly and properly. Brothers, what we long for is indeed holy and sublime. As priests, we have been called to this duty on trust. May we never be found wanting but vigilant as ever.[24]

---

[24] Being a homily delivered at Mass in the chapel of St. Paul College Seminary, Gbarnga, Liberia, Wednesday, twenty-ninth week in ordinary time, Ephesians 3:2–12, Luke 12:39–48, October 22.

Saints Simon and Jude

Be a good child, and God will help you.
St. Joan of Arc

WE CELEBRATE TODAY, dear brothers, the feast of Saints Simon and Jude, whom we know were apostles of our Lord. We want to wish those who bear these names in our midst a happy feast day. Little is known of these two apostles, whose names are always linked in the gospel accounts. Simon is called "the Zealot" and Jude "the son of James." However, our readings are quite instructive. Scripture scholars indicate that our first reading is "household codes," which were adapted from the Greco-Roman popular philosophy by New Testament scholars to assist in the moral instruction of Christians. In the New Testament, specifically, Christian motivation is presented as the basis for the imperatives expressed in the code. Principally, Christ's lordship over the body is presented as a model for the husband as the head of the wife. It is further expressed in Christ's love for the church and the image of the church as the bride of Christ. This spills from the background of the ancient Near Eastern sacred marriage of the gods. No wonder the author of Ephesians adapts Jesus as the bridegroom who cleanses the church, his bride, in the waters of baptism, so that clothed in her dowry of holiness and purity, she may now appear before him. As priests and seminarians, we stand to make manifest these roles of head and love for our bride the church. Tradition has it that the apostles all suffered various forms of martyrdom for the love they had for the faith. Similarly, may our resolves be strengthened by their faith.

In the gospel text, the parables about the kingdom do not stress the contrast between the smallness of the beginning and the greatness of the end product. What shone in the limelight is the growth that eventually takes place. It is a comfort to disciples like us who, as we continue our master's journey, will also face fierce opposition. In the kingdom, Jesus proclaims in words and deed that there is an epiphany of God for those who open their eyes and ears to see and hear it. We, as disciples of Christ, should be confident that God's kingdom, like the powerful corrupting agent, leaven, is operative and will achieve its goal despite all indications to the contrary. Like the psalmist this morning proclaims, "O blessed are those who fear the Lord and work in his ways." May those of us who truly aspire to walk in his ways find the strength to be heads and proud bridegrooms for the church.[25]

---

[25] Being a homily delivered in the chapel of St. Paul College Seminary, Gbarnga, Bong County, Liberia, thirtieth week, Ephesians 5:21–33; Luke 13:18–21, October 28, 2008.

Men of Irreproachable Character

To one who has faith, no explanation is necessary. To
one without faith, no explanation is possible.
St. Thomas Aquinas

WE CELEBRATE TODAY the memory of St. Leo the Great, pope and doctor of the church. Among the church's wonderful array of holy fathers, only a few are noted for being "the great," and today St. Leo is one of those. As we honor the memory of this great saint, may we also model our lives according to the noble teachings and rich legacies that he left behind. Let us ponder for a while his amazing profile. Elected pope in AD 440, he consolidated the organization of the church and its governments from Rome at a time of civil and doctrinal disorder. Attila's invasion was threatening, and the Monophysite heresy was abroad. However, he championed Christianity in this period. Many of his sermons and letters survive and reveal him as a man of clear, forceful intellect and faith. He died about AD 461. Our first reading has this to say of Christians—importantly of those who aspire for service in the church. We are servants of God, in fact, God's representatives, so we must be irreproachable, never arrogant or hot tempered, not heavy drinkers, not violent, and not out to make money. It goes further to add that one should be hospitable and a friend of all that is good, sensible, moral, devout, and self-controlled and have a firm grasp of the unchanging message of tradition, so as to be counted on for both expounding sound doctrine and refuting those who argue against it. This looks like a tall order for us all as we aspire and strive to live this noble calling as servants of God.

But the gospel reading today projects our Lord Jesus teaching his apostle in this discourse to pray for the increase of faith: " It would be better for you if a millstone were hung around your neck and you were thrown into the sea than for you to cause one of these little ones to stumble,"(Luke 17:2). Watch yourself. Personally, I believe that humility in whatever service we carry out for God is an all-important attitude and frame of mind. Strengthening one's faith would mean to perfect what is lacking in us. It could also connote the discovery of faith made clearer, a desire made stronger. It may also stand for the dependence of faith being made firmer and more fixed, a dedication of faith more entire and resolute, a delight of faith more pleasing, and a lot more. But I say in humility we offer this desire of pure faith to God in prayer, for it will be terrible for us if we are found wanting in our mission, as priests and aspiring priests.

The gospel is quick to remind us once more that "if your brother does something wrong, reprove him, and if he is sorry, forgive him. For if your faith were the size of a mustard seed, you would do great things." We all know the popular saying that "to ere is human but to forgive is divine." We need to forgive and especially be careful of what we say at times of anger. It behooves us to bring out the best in everyone, to cultivate a forgiving spirit, and forgive injury also, no matter how recent. I say this because this is the duty charged to those who are especially called to this noble ministry. May the irreproachable character that is preached be our ideal so that we all can manifest this wonderful spirit that distinguished the great pope and all the apostles we speak of at all times. Our responsorial psalm says, "Such are the men who seek your face, O Lord." This is my prayer, but most of all, this is our collective challenge.[26]

---

[26] Being a homily delivered at the chapel of St. Paul's College Seminary, Gbarnga, Bong County, Liberia, Monday, thirty-third week in ordinary time, Titus 1:1–9, Luke 17:1–6, November 10, 2008.

Your Enxdurance Will
Win You Your Lives

Faith does not quench desire, but inflames it.
St. Thomas Aquinas

WE LIVE IN interesting times, and we are besieged by phenomenal developments and unpredictable circumstances. Reality experts advertise all kinds of theories that we often hear on our communication media. I am sure you have met with a few! They say, "Desperate circumstances demand desperate measures." It is not uncommon to see our young people, of whom we are no exception, literally on the verge of trying anything and everything that is available. So, dear brothers, as long as we live with all these conditions, which are all too familiar to us, we may need to hold on to our faith with the understanding that only our endurance will win us all our lives. Maybe a few concrete examples will underscore this endurance and challenge to our faith. We must perseveras long as less than four million people of different socioeconomic, religious, and ethnic backgrounds cannot peacefully and equitably coexist within 43,000 square miles without resorting to recurring violence as a preferred option for transformation of conflicts:

as long as there is diminished capacity of government to provide quality education, health care, and other social services for the Liberian people

as long as there are needs to maintain advocacy and effective media use to address our prevailing situation characterized by illiteracy, poverty, and disease of pandemic proportions (HIV/AIDS, malaria, and TB)

as long as we acknowledge our need to direct attention and resources to achieve active participation of all stakeholders, gender equality, and poverty reduction in Liberia, Africa, and worldwide

as long as there are still visible signs of anger, prejudice, greed, insensitivity, and intolerance, which will continue to hinder our collective shift of mind, body, and spirit toward an inclusive, moral, disciplined, responsive, and responsible society

This list can be expanded upon, and we may not finish naming the ills of our society. It behooves those of us who, by the grace of God, have been called to his service to be able to concretely address these issues whenever and wherever we may find ourselves. This noble task begins now and within the given circumstance of our lives. As champions of our faith, but most of all, as custodians of the deeper mysteries of our Lord, it is only natural that we should continue to draw on each other's awareness of the implications of our tasks. The Lord assures us today that not a single hair of our heads will be lost on account of his name despite the many hazards of our noble callings. We all want to sing hymns for God when we eventually meet with him, but the melodies of these hymns begin from here. May we be ever resolved today to hold firm to this faith and win a crown of glory at the end of our stay.[27]

---

[27] Being a homily at Mass at the seminary chapel of St. Paul College Seminary, Gbarnga, Bong County, Liberia, thirty-fourth week in ordinary time, Revelation 15:1–4, Luke 21:12–19, Wednesday, November 26, 2008.

The Lord Will Wipe Away the Tears from Every Cheek

Pray, hope, and don't worry.
St. Pio of Pietrelina

AGAINST A BACKDROP of waiting in prayer and intense preparation, which Advent calls us to, we have from the readings this day a picture of a moving and rewarding experience. We all have been called to a special banquet, which the Lord himself has prepared for us—to put it into context, a celebration of his divine kingship. It is universal and very inclusive; it is placed within the understanding that death will be destroyed forever, that every tear will be wiped away from our cheeks, and our shame will be rubbed off completely. So reassuring is this reading today that we only have to revisit our daily situations in life and count ourselves lucky if we have to respond to this invitation. As we prepare for the Lord's coming, the mood in town has changed radically. The air is about preparation, but the commercial sales are dictating the tone of things. Prices will continue to soar, family resources will definitely be challenged, and relationships will be dependent on how much you will be ready to part with at this period of yuletide. The Lord alone is calling us to his banquet, a Eucharistic meal set in the most important period of the church's calendar, to prepare for his coming.

As expected, the gospel reading strengthens this picture when we discover that the events leading to the feeding of the crowds were preceded by the picture of healing, the astonishment of the crowds, the restoration of people's sight, the lame walking, and God being praised in the situation by all. This clearly is an event motivated by the compassion of Jesus as he takes the initiative of feeding the people. After inquiries that resulted in finding food, he gave thanks to God for the little that was offered. At the end came the miracle of feeding the multitude, and the leftovers filled seven baskets. This recalls not only the nation of Canaan but the universalistic approach of the first reading where we all have been invited to this banquet, this significant social event. Even as I speak, the point must be made that we all have been called to this feast, from different nations, with our peculiar backgrounds and roots, our different styles and persuasions, the different shades of opinions, our different colors and outlooks, our most intense pains and worries, but most of all, the shared delights of being considered for this awesome responsibility of championing the Lord's works among his people. These were the thoughts in the mind of the great patron of the mission as he was called when he set sail to the mission for which he dedicatedly gave his life and passionately answered God's call with. St. Francis Xavier was indeed a missionary who drew all peoples to this universal banquet, which the Lord is calling all of us to today. No matter the situation, he will be there to wipe away our tears and fill us with his love. We only need to respond to this call with the zeal and courage that the Lord alone wants for his Shepherd. Our interest may be particular, but the Lord's call is universal. There is no more opportune time than this Advent season.[28]

---

[28] Being a homily delivered at Mass in the seminary chapel of St. Paul's College Seminary, Gbarnga, Bong County, Liberia, first week of Advent, Isaiah 25:6–10, Matthew 15:29–37, Wednesday, December 3, 2008.

Do Not Be Afraid,
I Will Help You

Tribulation is a gift from God, one that he
especially gives His special friends.
St. Thomas More

A S WE CELEBRATE this Mass today, the astonishing
assurance that we receive from God should make us ever
ready and resolved to carry out anew our responsibilities. The
Lord himself is ready to help us and wants to dispel our fear. What are
these fears, and to what extent have they held us hostage and bound
us to them such that we are not ready to dispose of them. The Lord
himself is aware of our longing for his presence and senses that we
are not ready to do away with these fears. I must say that the world we
live in every day exposes us to these fears, and to be candid, they are
legion. Not only are we waking up to face a financial crisis that has
led to an economic recession across the globe, but we are also faced
these days with the threats of terror everywhere. It comes in terrorists'
attacks—the hijacking of planes, hotels, and the like—climatic changes
and natural disasters, and so on. The list can be endless. On the home
front, we see daily how people are dying from lack of medical care
because of our leaders' inordinate desire to hold on to power, leaders
who have refused to come to terms with certain prevailing realities

because of their desire to remain in the affairs of government. All this disillusionment and much more are a constant reminder of our fears and the fallen nature of man. They may seem distant from us, but we are constantly reminded that it may just be behind or next door to us.

Therefore, with an assurance from the Lord this morning to the Israelites, "I will help you," I think we who are also products of this divine history have a reason to celebrate that the Lord will come to our aid. He wants to do this not just because he wants to save us but because he is bound to us. On our part, we have to do away with our inordinate desires and wants and the relentless search and longing for the worthless things that this material world offers. We need to invest our resources and channel our energies to the glories of the Lord, which he wants to offer us. This period is just about the best time to begin to explore this route. The Lord wants to be part of our desire for him; he wants us to be walking the difficult part of life with him. He wants to be part of the discoveries of our vocation and the growth in our spiritual journey. Ultimately, he wants to come to our aid and save us. As we embark on this journey of self-discovery and the need to pay attention to the activities that will bring us closer to God at this period of preparation, may I urge you to open your eyes to the realities of this time and see what the Lord himself is calling us to! We may have eyes, but if we are not careful, it will be difficult for us to inspire confidence in others. Let us not be afraid to make that bold step that calls for a complete change of heart, so that when the Lord comes, we will be ready to share in his glories.[29]

---

[29] Being a homily delivered at the seminary chapel of St. Paul's College Seminary, Gbarnga, Bong County, Republic of Liberia, second week of Advent (B), Thursday, Isaiah 41:13–20, Matthew 11:11–15, December 11, 2008.

Choose Life, So That You ... May Live in the Love of the Lord

You learn to speak by speaking, to study by studying, to run by
running, to work by working, and just so, you learn to love by loving.
All those who think to learn in any other way deceive themselves.
St. Francis de Sales

PART OF THE excitement of the Lenten season is the constant
reminder of a need to retrace our steps to the real meaning
and significance of life. Today, a choice is placed before the
children of Israel, whose descendants we are, to choose life so that
they and invariably we will live in the love of the Lord. This love of
the Lord has made us to abstain, refrain, withhold, and withdraw from
doing so many things. Above all, we are obeying the voice of the Lord,
clinging to him and not relenting in preserving his ways. This period
presents us with this wonderful opportunity. We must choose today
to live this life as priests and seminarians to the full. It is not a life of
half measures, and we don't have the luxury of an embattled life, filled
with tension, distortions, provocations, and blatant neglect. Ours is
a choice of living the life our Lord has called us to in its fullness, its
totality, and its entirety.

In the pursuit of this life, we may need to give up so much; we may have to carry our crosses day by day as we advance on our journey to the Lord. In renouncing ourselves, we may have to put up with the pains of a nagging brother, the absurdities of a roommate, the misdirection of a pious colleague, or, most of all, the plain unbelief of a deviant in a cassock! It seems the challenge of renouncing oneself for the Lord is daunting, but the Lord insists that a life lost in the battles of staying decent and remaining focused is a life gained. This is simply because the intent is for our Lord Jesus Christ. No matter what the world offers, let us remember that the Lord offers more—be it intelligence, beauty, or the sophistication of this world. So let us crave to choose life and live it in the Lord. May our Lenten observances and this period of an intense spiritual journey redirect our lives to remaining and staying decent for the Lord.[30]

---

[30] Being a homily delivered at Mass at the seminary chapel of St. Paul College Seminary, Gbarnga, Bong County, Republic of Liberia, Friday after Ash Wednesday, Ezekiel 18:21–28, Matthew 5:20–26, February 27, 2009.

My Confessions

O Master, make me chaste, but not yet!
St. Augustine

I DO HAVE A confession to make. This is made with the understanding that I will come to appreciate deeply and immensely God's wonderful gifts to me. If the roles we play are reversed and you, dear brothers, have the pulpit, understandably, you may want to give it out that the scriptures admonish us to do unto others what we want done to us. You may stress also the significance of asking with a sincere heart, just like Queen Esther this morning, who seeks the wisdom, counsel, and protection of God. Similarly, the gospel too places emphasis on this aspect of asking. In comparison, therefore, if we who are humans can do good things, how much more our father in heaven? One thing is clear; the question of attitude is heavily prized. You may want to show what sort of attitude we place before God when we ask for things.

This period presents us with the opportunity to truly cleanse ourselves of all distorted versions of self, purge ourselves of sins, so that with a contrite heart and spirit, we can ask anything of the Lord and it will be granted. My confession, therefore, is that I am truly and adequately sure at this opportune time that I can with a sincere heart ask the Lord for anything, given the many aspects of my dysfunctional life. The truth is as the psalmist reads, "On the day I called, you answered me..." (Psalm 138:3) I may have to make this call and take that bold step for God. He will certainly answer us. It may be an exaggerated feeling of inadequacy! He has answered already. A false sense of guilt? He has sufficiently ennobled us. It may be a deep and profound admittance to him, like I had this morning. In all, it is the Lord who is speaking to us. We come to him with a pure heart. This is my confession. What is yours?[31]

---

[31] Being a homily delivered at Mass at the seminary chapel of St. Paul's College Seminary, Gbarnga, Bong County, Republic of Liberia, Thursday, first week of Lent, Esther 4:17, Matthew 7:7–12, March 5, 2009.

Being Humbled and Being Exalted

This is the very perfection of a man, to
find out his own imperfections.
St. Augustine

D EAR BROTHERS, IN my ministry as a priest, I have been
very careful in discussing the Pharisees. Today, I am still
cautioned by experience. I will only take up issues with them,
just like our Lord himself draws our attention to it this morning. They
occupy a significant place in the hierarchy of Judaism and should be
listened to. However, they do not practice what they preach. Our
Lord's confrontation with the Pharisees was centered on their insisting
that others should do the right thing while failing to lead in the same
direction, seeking recognition and attention, attracting significance by
wanting to be noticed, and most of all placing emphasis on titles.

We all agree with that wise saying that "an unexamined life is not
worth living." As we do our conscious examination this morning,
should we not be asking ourselves this pointed question: How many
times have we insisted that others should do the right thing and have
failed in taking steps to lead in such direction? If we insist that someone
should forgive, what steps have we taken to ensure that the forgiveness
we seek yields the required result? When we cry foul play and insist that

we are right and we alone should be listened to, are we much different from the Pharisees? The message of our Lord as it comes down hard on the Pharisees this morning should serve as a warning to us too, especially as we adorn ourselves with beautiful dresses and occupy a privileged position in this church. Our Lenten retreat should exalt us to humility so that we would be exalted. By this gospel, I know that I have been totally subdued. I see myself drowning, and like in the first reading from Isaiah, I seek to "wash, make myself clean and take my wrongdoing out of God's sight."[32]

---

[32] Being a homily delivered at Mass at the Seminary Chapel of St. Paul's College Seminary, Gbarnga, Bong County, Republic of Liberia, Tuesday, second week of Lent, Isaiah 1:10, 16–20; Matthew 23:1–12, March 10, 2009.

A New Heaven and
a New Earth

To live is to change, and to be perfect is to have changed often.
Bl. John Henry Cardinal Newman

ALL AROUND US, dear brothers, we hear revealing news of change, a new approach to doing things, a fresh start, an opportunity, a chance of a lifetime. New strategies, breaking new ground, adopting a new stand, taking exceptional new steps, plunging into new territories—the language is clear and simple enough; it seems to suggest that we have once again an occasion for renewal. No wonder the language of the scriptures this morning from the prophet Isaiah shows no difference; in fact, it is quite revealing.

For I am about to create new heavens and a new earth; the former things shall not be remembered or come to mind. But be glad and rejoice forever in what I am creating; for I am about to create Jerusalem as a joy, and its people as a delight. I will rejoice in Jerusalem, and delight in my people; no more shall the sound of weeping be heard in it, or the cry of distress. (Isaiah 65:17–19)

With such an amazing clarity from the prophets this morning, the Lenten period continues in the same drama and language to repeatedly task us daily in our most cherished efforts to return to God, through prayers, fasting, and abstinence but most importantly through a new us. With what eyes do I see this new challenge? With what language am I hearing, and how am I responding to this period? Am I changing for the better in Christian life, as a seminarian in formation, as a priest under holy orders, or am I asking for signs and making unrealistic demands, chasing illusive dreams and building castles in the air? Our Lord in the gospels this morning reminds us that those who insist on signs and portents before believing should beware.

The court official and his family believed in a show of deep, personal, and profound faith in the Lord after that miraculous cure, but we may not need to ask about signs. In fact, our belief is uttermost; the quality of our belief should be expressed in this new language, new expressions that have paved our society. The quality of our renewal should radiate in the way we handle the week ahead, our appearance, our discussions, our engagements, and most of all our prayers. This gives a good showing of our belief, engages above all our Lenten observances. It is our desire as we look toward Easter that our prolonged Lenten retreats should bring us up to a new heaven and a new earth—an Easter people, a New Jerusalem to be its joy and my people's gladness![33]

---

[33] Being a homily delivered at Mass at the seminary chapel of St. Paul College Seminary, Gbarnga, Bong County, Republic of Liberia, Monday, fourth week of Lent, Isaiah 65:17–21, John 4:43–54, March 23, 2009.

A Sad Day for Elders ...

Temperance is a disposition that restrains our
desires for things which it is base to desire.
St. Augustine

DEAR BROTHERS, STATEMENTS have been made on these readings before, and now as I reflect on it, I am even at loss as to how to place my thoughts. Many a thought has flashed through my mind since I chose to reflect on the issues that have presented themselves. As Africans, we consider that age is a prominent factor in the psychosexual development of an individual, and moreover, elders, whom God has blessed with wisdom and age, are considered very ably filled with maturity, discipline, and control. The cases we have before us in Africa would have to be considered an abomination and a desecration of the land. It would require a ritual cleansing to appease the gods, and those culprits will be condemned, expelled from the land, and banished. Clearly, it would seem that with Susanna, the elders in our story were at loss. They had been overcome by their emotions, and it took the best part of them. Remember the scriptures note that through these elders posing as judges, wickedness has come to Babylon.

Many questions may be asked, but it shows that one way in which we may quickly lose ourselves is if we are not in control of our emotions. While we take time to care for our physical needs through eating a healthy diet and keeping up mental and physical health, it seems safe to say that we may have to take time to address our emotional and spiritual needs as well. We see this morning that being charged with the responsibilities of keeping and protecting the laws, the elders became corrupt and selfish and displayed wanton disregard for everybody. They become lords to themselves and took undue advantage of the people and situations. This recklessness of the leaders expressed itself in all the fabric of society and became vividly showcased in Susanna's story. But for the intervention of the prophet Daniel, disaster would have fallen on Susanna and her family. The Lord heard her cry and prayers. A similar fate awaited the woman caught in the very act of adultery. It would seem the Pharisees and scribes were eager to justify their wrong dealings. So, they quickly put together this elegant display of crass stupidity. Again, our Lord's intervention saved the neck of the poor woman caught in the very act of committing adultery. It was a singularly sad day for the elders because Jesus's challenge struck deep down, when he observed, "If there is anyone without sin, let him be the first to throw a stone." John's gospel notes carefully that they started to go away one by one, beginning with the eldest. One thing is sure, the virtues that were associated with the elders at this instance were put to the test, and they became a curse rather than a blessing to the land. Jesus's intervention was bringing back that lost credibility, but it came with its consequences. It was because he did things like this that the elders were more resolved to kill him. As elders and aspiring elders, a reexamination of our respective selves is my word of caution, for any elder who lives in a glass house should not throw stones![34]

---

[34] Being a homily delivered at Mass in the chapel of St. Paul College Seminary, Gbarnga, Bong County, Republic of Liberia, Monday, fifth week of Easter, Daniel 13:1–9, 15–17, 19–30, 33–62; John 8:1–11, March 30, 2009.

Why Look among the Dead for Someone Who Is Alive?

Ignorance of Scripture is ignorance of Christ.

St. Jerome

OR THE BEST part of last night and for the better part of today, we carried gloomy faces and kept mute over the sadness that has befallen us. We had reached the climax of our mortification and prayers that seemed shattered by the blows of death. But as I speak, "the Lord is raised from the dead and all things are made anew!" Because of my strong belief in the power of the resurrection, I must say that I see in each of you, a new light and a new personality. In fact, I know that the whole world this night has been made anew. Each one of us is seen in a new light, because if one considers that moments earlier, at the beginning of the Mass, when darkness covered this place, it was obvious that we had to remain where we were because we were uncertain about what lay in front of us, behind us, or even before us. As we remained in darkness, all kinds of thoughts made their way through our heads. We may have known what to do, but we became unsure, because who will take the first step and blast us out of these inhibitions. But with light comes brightness, newness, elegance, and most of all, presence.

In the story of the resurrection, the drama that is truly exhibited is that a new world is founded; a new way of existing is inaugurated. Jesus Christ, our Lord, is risen. Christ lives! The resurrection of the Lord shows that bodily death is only the dream which proceeds a new day that has no sunset. Yes, the resurrection is "newness of life" (Romans 6:4). Jesus is "the resurrection and the life" (John 11:25). Brothers, we live in a world that etches its marks on our lives in a number of ways. It seeks relevance in all sorts of pseudo meanings. Some find life as defined in pleasure. As a result, they are surrounded with every conceivable thing of pleasure—luxury cars, homes, offices, women, and so on—and they are constantly in a perpetual search for pleasure. For others, it is power. They want to possess power by all means. Their lives are wrought with a constant longing for scheming, grabbing, accumulating, reaping benefits, and so on. For others still, it is wealth. They want it so much that they may not mind if all the wealth of the land is placed under their care to be dispensed at their will and caprice. Yes, they want to have and have all of it. After all, they too must have life, and they want it to the "full."

Brothers, it is not my intention on this holy night to drag you to the intricacies contained from the experience of the resurrection. Suffice it to say at this moment, in effect, for our interpretations of what Christ's resurrection means, we do have some solemn "magisterial" statements to guide us, but let us largely explore two other sources. These sources are the ordinary life and teachings of the church and the situation of life in the New Testament. Drawing from these two, therefore, one can safely say that in this very night, around us, we have experienced the power of the resurrection. Our lives must necessarily change.

It adds to the interest of us all to know where we are as regards the state of things in the development of our own spirituality. Let me remind you that it was the design of God that he would save his world and give it this new life. Many of us were already trapped in the world, as I have shown, by our tastes and cravings. The seductive glories of this world are still very much with us. Perhaps some of us are already short of nothing but dead in these longings. May the resurrection of the Lord provide an outlet for us! The angels observed, "Why look among the dead for someone who is alive?" Although we are caught by the sins of the world, the resurrection of our Lord has broken down those walls and barriers that threaten our advancement, spiritually, morally, and otherwise. From now on, we look at the world differently, as a redeemed people capable of all possibilities! They may be mental, economic, creative, academic, and so on. Impossible situations can become possible miracles. May the resurrective experience of this very night continue to brighten all of us to the very heights that the Lord wants us to go to.[35]

---

[35] Being a homily delivered at the Easter vigil at the chapel of St. Paul's College Seminary, Bong County, Republic of Liberia, April 11, 2009.

St. Joseph the Worker

To work is to Pray.
St. Benedict

WE COMMEMORATE TODAY the memorial of St. Joseph the Worker, patron of working people. This memorial was established by Pope Pius XII in 1955. Years ago, I was privileged to be asked a phenomenal question—or at least at that time, I thought it was really a question to ponder. I had this friend who had graduated from college and as is typical of all college graduates was all worked up about when he would begin to work and earn his first salary. As days progressed to weeks and months, eventually, it turned out that a year had passed, and the work never materialized. I saw in my friend the resignation and disillusionment that usually accompanies this sort of attitude. Not only was my friend mystified, but he seemed to be in a perpetual state of stupor. Once I accosted him with what I thought was a helpful suggestion, and the answer I got is the focus of my wonder this morning. "Donald! Do you know what it means to be in the house without a job or work?" I wasn't prepared for what I got, so I didn't really have an answer. Since I have never been in a situation without work, I may not be able to really fathom what my friend was going through. But what I can say for sure is that I hope I will not be in a situation where I may have to at any stage look for work. It is depressing, dehumanizing, degrading, difficult, and simply damaging.

The horrifying experiences of those who may have to go without work every day or those who have lost their jobs notwithstanding make one appreciate the fact that the church has over the years and through its history shown that to work is fundamental to the active development of man. On a day when we celebrate with those who work and those looking for jobs, to mention a few emerging thoughts may not be out of place. The creation story we have just heard justifies the absolute necessity of work and praises the creativity and imaginative prowess that come with work. In work, we experience the glory of God's creation. Consider carefully those melodious words packed with meaning that seem to refreshingly rhyme with every emphasis when we render that song,

O Lord, my God, when I am in awesome wonder, consider all the works thy hands have made! I see the stars; I hear the mighty thunder, the power throughout the universe displayed. Then sings my soul, my savior God, to thee, how great thou art, how great thou are … ("How Great Thou Art" Swedish folk melody, adapted by Stuart K. Hine, 1899-1989)

Yes! Indeed, we see in God an abiding need for work as it is expressed in his creative deeds. In Jesus too we trace a humble inheritance. This is the carpenter's son, surely? Even in the church's rich traditions, we remember the period when we all stopped for the angelus at midday, and work was seen as the measure of our own path to salvation, for an idle mind, they say, is the devil's workshop! The monks themselves quipped and correctly too that to work is to pray. Brothers, as we celebrate the joy of the worker, our prayers are with those who may go to sleep without work today. Our hearts and prayers are with them, and most of all for those who are charged with the responsibilities of ensuring that labor is created, may they all work for the benefit of many who need to work. For ourselves, too, we ask that we may find fulfillment in our labor as servants of God. Above all, may the intercession of St. Joseph be an everlasting guide.[36]

---

[36] Being a homily delivered on the memorial of St. Joseph the Worker at the seminary chapel of St. Paul's College Seminary, Gbarnga, Bong County, Republic of Liberia, third week of Easter, Genesis 1:26–2:3, Matthew 13:54–58, May 1, 2009.

Be Brave, I Have
Conquered the World

I know well that the greater and more beautiful the work is,
the more terrible will be the storms that rage against it.
St. Faustina

A QUICK GLANCE AT the mass media we have, be it print or electronic, every morning will suggest to you the amount of trouble one must put up with each day. It runs from every facet of life. The government of the day comes under intense pressure over its policies, resulting in massive protests from all walks of life. This will usually lead to a crippling of an already embittered organization, enormous suffering under the weight of reckless spending, and poor decisions in planning and administration. I am sure you will be glad to fill in the gaps for me if I dare ask for suggestions. How about news on the home front? We are daily besieged with all sorts of violence, recklessness, hopelessness, and pain that seem to be the lot that has characterized the modern family on the home front. Topmost of these are domestic violence, wife battering, rape, drugs, indiscriminate shooting, kidnapping, and so on. Recent surveys indicate that suicide figures, even here in Africa, are on the rise. The reasons of course are largely the seeming hopelessness of a great majority who are lost in the gore of what is our life today.

Brothers, indeed, the problems of the world are many, in contrast to the beauty and wonder of God's creation. Our Lord Jesus's admonition this morning to be brave, for he has conquered the world should be viewed from every context with a positive desire to overcome this challenge that our world continues to pose to us—not only as Christians, seminarians, and priests but most of all as humans who inhabit the whole world with its joys and sorrows, funs and thrills, pains and passions, love and hate. As we prepare for the coming of the Holy Spirit, we are reminded of the works of the spirit like the men in this morning's readings. They began to speak in tongues when they received baptism. Their boldness and persuasion not only remains a thing of admiration but stands worthy of emulation.

Yes, we must be bold to proclaim this good news in all situations of life. Let us not pick and choose. For when it suits us, we are courageous and confronting, but when it hurts us, we chicken out in mediocrity and aloofness. Jesus reminds us that although we may scatter and each go his or her separate way at times, it is only in him will we find peace. Despite the troubles of this world, may we continue to press on in his name, for we are indeed conquerors in the one who has chosen and sent us![37]

---

[37] Being a homily delivered at Mass at the seminary chapel of St. Paul College Seminary, Gbarnga, Bong County, Republic of Liberia, seventh week of Easter, Acts of the Apostles 19:1–8, John 16:29–33, Monday, May 25, 2009.

Keep and Teach

Listen and attend with the ear of your heart.
St. Benedict

A S A GENERAL rule, we are expected to keep, uphold, and teach the basic moral rules required to run homes, rectories, parishes, and establishments of all sorts and, most of all, how to manage our own lives. When it comes to the practice of this basic moral rule, it lives to be desired. As a result, we have grown accustomed to seeing in our daily encounters unhealthy situations where these rules of life are flaunted, disregarded, ridiculed, and made fun of in public as well as in private. As we wonder, the situation festers so much so that we are now experiencing a dearth of social mishaps that is threatening to run down our whole system. It is manifesting itself in family ties, social institutions, educational facilities, and governments. Above all, it has taken on our religious beliefs. While we mourn the debt that has robed us in this decay, we are admonished, dear brothers, today to keep and teach the commandments of God, for we will be considered great in heaven. One way of automatic admission to heaven by my reading of today's gospel is that once we keep and teach the commands of God, we will be allowed entry and also become great. In making heaven, therefore, we must begin right here on earth to eye heavenly benefits.

The task of keeping and teaching these commands of God is a mission that will be the exclusive preserve of future priests. It means that the preparation for these tasks must be intense, comprehensive, sacred, and holy. As administrators of the new covenant, seeking to keep what is most durable, I believe that we must develop the act of living in the presence of the spirit. We must become aware of the spirit's counsel, directions, orientations, and, most of all, love. May we cherish what we have received, faithfully guarding it and passing it on with all the love and trust that has been won with pride for us.[38]

---

[38] Being a homily delivered at Mass at the chapel of St. Paul College Seminary, Gbarnga, Bong County, Republic of Liberia, Wednesday, tenth week in ordinary time, 2 Corinthians 3:4–1, Matthew 5:17–19, June 10, 2009.

Love Your Enemies

We must fear God out of love, not love Him out of fear.
Saint Francis de Sales

RECENTLY, I DREW a line, making sure that the one I considered my enemy understood where I stood behind the line. If we came in contact at all, it stirred trouble and reactions. Having lived in this condition for a while, I was humbled by the gospel this morning, when once more the challenge of the gospel presented a comeback. Love your enemies. It looks difficult especially when you feel as I do that your enemy does not appreciate your love. The gospel is clear about you loving your enemy anyway. This is because this is an exceptional thing to do. There is no room for rationalization, escapism, or projections! All that is expected, especially for us priests and future priests, is to love the enemy so that we become perfect as our heavenly father is perfect.

Who then is the enemy? It maybe the boy next door, your neighbor whom you have shared so much with, especially tense moments, impossible situations, the one whose failure you have championed, whom you have conspired against, who drives you nuts, creates ghost pimples in you, and increases your blood pressure. We are admonished to love him. One may say the gospel presents such an impossible task. The reason is because we have chosen to do it the human way. Let us try the master's way. He maintains that we not only love but pray for those who persecute us. In this way, we will be sons of our father in heaven. As a result, I have earmarked a praying strategy to fire my enemies with heavenly prayers and truly ask God to hear these prayers because if he does not do battle on my behalf, I may fail in the mission of loving my enemies. Brothers, let us therefore continue to pray for the strength to carry out this mission of Christ faithfully with peace and love, for we want to be perfect like our heavenly father is.[39]

---

[39] Being a homily delivered at Mass in the chapel of St. Paul College Seminary, Gbarnga, Republic of Liberia, Tuesday, eleventh week in ordinary time, 2 Corinthians 8:1–9, Matthew 5:43–48, June 16, 2009.

You Are Worth More Than a Hundred Sparrows

Devotion is a certain act of the will by which man
gives himself promptly to divine service.
St. Thomas Aquinas

THIS IS A great moment of history when the church gathers to reflect on issues relating to justice, peace, and reconciliation in Africa. It offers us a unique opportunity to reflect on this simple but profound understanding that the church of Africa and its children are also "worth more than hundreds of sparrows." As we await the outcome of the synod proceedings at this great period of intense interest in the priests and our priesthood, permit me to say a few pertinent words. We are children of faith like the first reading reminds us this morning, and it is this faith in God that makes us happy when the Lord considers us as sinless. This is important because we can only make that boast if we are noted to be sinless. Should it not be the case that as we pursue all the activities that take place in this place we can candidly make the comments that happy are the priests and seminarians for we are people of peace, justice, and reconciliation. Similarly, we enjoy the unique confraternity that makes us people of God. Surely our daily efforts at these ideals will make us righteous in the sight of God.

However, here is the caution of our Lord to his apostle this morning that is worth pondering and should be taken with meticulous care. The Pharisee makes religion a profession and becomes dangerously hypocritical in his dealings with people. I think it is proper that as priests and seminarians, we should try to guard against this form of behavior and practice because we ourselves may sometimes fall in the same sins and crimes of the Pharisees. For our Lord to describe this as a "leaven" means that it may puff us with pride, embitter us with malice, and make our service unacceptable. So we must be wary of imitating the Pharisees and be careful in our dealings with people. Other times, it seems so natural to include a little lie, for it will not hurt so much, as the thinking may go, but it is important to remember that a "lying tongue is but for a moment." We are people of God, and we must fear and respect God always. He knows our abilities and capacities. We glory in the understanding that he watches over us and fronts our causes. He is our refuge and will fill us with the joy of his salvation. The message for all of us is that we should throw away this hypocrisy and pursue righteousness with a clear heart. We should champion honesty, industry, and generosity but above all the commitment to excellence for which we are all known. As we await the outcome of the synod and savor the sweetness of the year of the priest, may the good Lord be with and bless his words in our hearts.[40]

---

[40] Being a homily delivered at Mass in the chapel of St. Paul College Seminary, Gbarnga, Bong County, Republic of Liberia, Friday, twenty-eighth week in ordinary time, Romans 4:1–8, Luke 12:1–7, October 16, 2009.

A Great Deal Is
Given on Trust

Patience is the companion of wisdom.
St. Augustine

D EAR BROTHERS, IT is quite clear that a lot has been
entrusted to us as religious leaders and the keepers of the
proud possession of our religious heritage. We are truly the
custodians and guidance of the treasure and wealth of our church. It
means that we are chosen and have been given a great deal on trust.
Believe it or not, a lot has been placed on us, and today we are reminded
of this noble responsibility. We are to keep watch and be vigilant and to
go about our duty diligently while awaiting the return of the master. Is
it the case that we are truly keeping watch, or are we buying time while
the flock has wandered far away and we have no trace? Or have we been
overpowered by the enemy and the flock stolen from us? The answer to
these questions while we ponder them begins here in the seminary, in
the vigilance that we may exhibit in the way we carry out our assigned
duties, in the manner and grace with which we manage time, for
everything is very important and could be considered carefully as a
dress rehearsal for future promise.

Another interesting theme is knowing the will of the father and
doing it. This will attracts future rewards and benefits as the readings

suggest this morning. However, if this will of the father is not known, we may find that we will only increase the anger and the wrath of the one who has put us on this mission. Is it not the case that a lot of us do not know the will of the master? We carry on as if to say we are up and about the master's will while in essence we are only wallowing in abject confusion and tension. The first reading warns us of the dangers of sin and how once we allow our bodies to become the attention of sin it becomes very difficult to pull out. Rather we are slaves to these sins. The sins of the flesh are many and varied. They come in droves and may be very contagious—the lure of going out and having just one for the road as we usually say, the pleasure of sharing the good times with old friends and forgetting the assigned duty allotted to us on the campus, the temptation of taking charge of some affairs with the stated objective that you are also a priest in training, and similar odd interventions! This, to my mind, is not knowing the wishes of the master; it is carrying out our own wishes. Remember, we are to feed the household of God with all the ingredients of a servant. This and only this is the work we have been asked to do, and happy are those servants whom the Lord finds at his employment. Remember, we have been put in charge based on trust, and it is this trust that the Lord wants to see manifest in us as leaders and bearers of this deposit of faith. May we never be found wanting in our resolve to carry out the Lord's mission.[41]

---

[41] Being a homily delivered at Mass in the seminary chapel of St. Paul College Seminary, Gbarnga, Republic of Liberia, Wednesday, twenty-ninth week in ordinary time, Romans 6:12–18, Luke 12:39–48, October 21, 2009.

Render an Account of
Your Stewardship

Be kind to all and severe to thyself.
St. Teresa of Avila

D EAR BROTHERS, THE readings of today, especially the
gospels, never stop fascinating me. Each time I reflect on
their importance, they speak volumes. It only goes to show
how utterly awesome the scriptures have remained as a spiritual book
for all times. Here is a dishonest steward who is asked to render his
accounts. The master has heard from other quarters how he is carrying
out his duties. Quickly, our brother knows now that he is in for real
trouble and wants to remain relevant, so he finds his way back to the
heart of his master. The best possible option is to devise new strategies
of coping with the situation. The first is to win the hearts of those
whom he has offended and does not seem to know. He gets interested
in the plight of those whom, before now, he never considered to be of
importance, only agents to be used and dumped at his disposal. How
ingenious! This is what he does: first, by calling each debtor, sitting
down with him or her, and finding how to be relevant to both the
debtor and the debt, he endears himself to them, and at the end, he
wins the admiration of both the master and the debtors. How is that
for using what you have to get what you want?

We too, dear brothers, will have to render our accounts someday to the master, who has placed us at his service. How bold are we going to be when asked how we have performed our service? Have we been selective of whom to deal with at the expense of others? Are we picking and choosing and only committing to memory those for whom we feel we owe more a debt than a duty? Is the quality of our service and care noticeable, or is it despised and people would rather not be with us? What is the commitment level of our service delivery? Are we able to go the extra mile like St. Paul this morning, who insisted on carrying the message of Christ to other lands where Christ was not known? For Christians, having seen and heard us, is the agitation for Christ still pertinent in their lives, or are people just waiting for us to conclude our polite talk, so that they can carry out their best wishes? The dishonest servant understood where he belonged in the equation of things and wanted a balance especially knowing that he was going to face a consequence. Shouldn't it be the case that we too would be able to say that we understand, having lived with our people, and that we can truly say that this is it? Brothers, the Lord has shown us his salvation like the psalmist intones this morning. We know the way to the father, and he wants us to lead others to him. We speak the language of today and are wise in the affairs of our time. Let us therefore use all that is available to us as Christians, seminarians, and priests to bring this salvation to all. Who knows? We too may be praised for our efforts.[42]

---

[42] Being a homily delivered at the seminary chapel of St. Paul's College Seminary, Gbarnga, Bong County, Republic of Liberia, Friday, thirty-first week in ordinary time, Romans 15:14–21, Luke 16:1–8, November 6, 2009.

Christ the Universal King

We judge all things according to the divine truth.
St. Augustine

T HE CONCEPT OF kingship is slowly dying in our midst. The simple reason is that as a system of governance, monarchy has today lost its relevance in several cultures and communities. What we have is democracy. Democracy as a system of governance has suddenly, within these last two centuries, built its way into existence and seems to hold more currency, especially today. As a result of this shift in paradigm, the understanding of kingship seems to be reserved for books of literature and history. Those who are more adventurous may encounter it in some existing cultures that are spread over Africa and some parts of the world. Since the reading of today permits us to say a thing or two about kingship, let me devote a few moments to exploring the basis for kingship as we know it among our people. The very first point of interest is how sovereignty was recognized and understood. It is common knowledge, or rather sources tell us, that sovereignty comes from God. After all, it is God himself who created the world. He in turn handed it over to man to be inhabited and enjoyed.

Anthropologically speaking, as man evolved over the centuries and similarly, as communities emerged, systems and cultures developed along various lines, lineages, and backgrounds. The stories of how these various cultures of the world began to take root and rose to preeminence are recorded in the holy writs, scriptures, and histories of the various literary cultures of the world. However, others developed orally through myths, legends, and stories. A lot of this information we have come to know from our various forms and sources of study—archaeology, ethnology, paleontology, and so on. The fact is, brothers, that kingship as a form of governance became the other form of rule at one point in our history. We recall with nostalgia the great kingdoms of the Benin, Songhai, and Mali empires in the West Coast and the great kingdoms of Zimbabwe in the south coast of our beloved continent. The elements of kingship were tied with the sovereignty that was conferred to the king and his household. This was done as a form of leadership for the people and land. The king was/is chief custodian of the rich treasures of the land. He was also the one who provided security for the land and had the last say on matters relating to peace and stability in the land. Robed in royal splendor, he was the proud possessor of the ancestral heritage of the land both in spirit and in kind. The rest of what kingship stood for and how a king is vested, appointed, and enthroned is well known to you.

Since this is so familiar to some of us, it comes as no surprise, therefore, that today we celebrate the universal kingship of our Lord on this last Sunday of the year. The first reading reminds us that this vision of the kingship of our Lord was known and preached during the time of Daniel and must have been familiar to all. The second reading tells us that the Lord himself is the beginning and the end of all that there is. Our Lord Jesus Christ is the firstborn from the dead and the ruler of the kings of the earth. While the gospel reading maintains that his kingdom is not of this world, however, he is a king, and it is for this reason that he came into the world.

There are no questions on the authority of our Lord. He, however, showed us the best way to be a king in the world to come. Whether this is applicable to our situation is the challenge we have to face as leaders or those destined to be leaders someday. Sovereignty will be laid on us, and we will be expected to lead our people to the right path of righteousness, peace, and prosperity. What is the attitude that should accompany those who may be chosen for these humbling tasks expected of a leader in the fashion of a king? The most challenging part of it all is we live in an age when there seems to be a lot of anguish poured on leaders who don't deliver on their promises. The answer to this question is clear, my brothers, from the standpoint of our Lord. He came for the truth, and anyone who is committed to the truth should hear his voice. We too are people of truth, or at least we are committed to the truth. We know his voice and are ready to hear it. We pray, therefore, that our leaders or those in leadership positions of the world will be people committed to the truth. They will pursue the truth and in turn administer it with love and care. We pray for ourselves that in our formation process, we will work in furtherance of the truth and be champions of these truths in our respected positions. May the celebration of Christ the King be a sure reminder of our stand today and always![43]

---

[43] Being a homily delivered at the seminary chapel of St. Paul Seminary, Gbarnga, Bong County, Republic of Liberia, last Sunday of the year (B), Daniel 7:13–14, Revelation 1:5–8, John 18:33–37.

According to Your Faith, Let This Be Done

For Faith, is the beginning and the end is love, and God is the two of them brought into unity. After these comes whatever else makes up a Christian gentleman.
St. Ignatius of Antioch

DEAR BROTHERS, WE are no strangers to a scene where we have felt very sympathetic to the victims concerned and are helpless or incapacitated in doing anything. It may be an accident scene where a loved one is down with a spinal cord injury. Or one comes in contact with a patient at an emergency ward of a general hospital with both legs hanging in the air. Moved with compassion and desiring to help but still finding oneself completely helpless in this rather difficult situation is challenging. The lists of the difficulties that daily plague us are so numerous that it may look like there is no end to it. But this is what the advent season does to us that as we await the coming of the Lord, the messianic message is insisted on rather strongly. A time will come when what seems to be almost an impossibility become a possibility in the person of the messiah.

The first reading today tells of the day when the deaf will hear the words of a book and after shadow and darkness the eyes of the blind will see. And the gospel reading is quick to manifest this message in the cure of the two blind men in Matthew's story whose faith had saved them. Yes, dear brothers, faith in our Lord brings not just healing but salvation to those who admit to this faith. Therefore, as we await the coming of the messiah, how about the many times in our own lives when we have felt we could do it on our own, when we felt the intervention of others is not necessary and most certainly not called for? What about those times when we felt let down by family and friends and the last thing we wanted to do was to submit ourselves again to the same fate? Many of us just prefer to be lone rangers and would rather struggle on our own than imagine the assistance of another betrayal. These thoughts, wide as they are, represent in a sampling, the way we respond individually to the call of God. But today we are reminded that to those who call on the Lord and believe that he can do this, he will surely respond appropriately. So as we prepare to receive the coming of our Lord, should it not be the case that we intensify our belief in him—be it in our struggles with relationships, work, studies, the entire formation process, colleagues, and most of all our own selves? Let us commend them to God, and like the blind man in our readings this morning, he will grant us our heart's desire and strengthen us in our search for him.[44]

---

[44] Being a homily delivered at the seminary chapel of St. Paul College Seminary, Gbarnga, Bong County, Liberia, Friday, first week of Advent, Isaiah 29:17–24, Matthew 9:27–31, December 3, 2009.

Speak, Lord, Your Servant Is Listening

> Great are those two gifts, wisdom and continence: wisdom,
> forsooth, whereby we are formed in the knowledge of God;
> continence whereby we are not conformed to this world.
> St. Augustine

D EAR BROTHERS, THE world today has a lot of pressures, and to try recounting the kinds of worries or occasions one has to do serious battle with may be an exercise in futility. This is so because we all at one time or another are faced with a number of troubles constantly. That is why the virtue of listening becomes very important, dramatic, and apt. This kind of listening, in particular the kind we experience the young Samuel engaged in, comes with assistance and training. On his own, the young Samuel may have been at loss to understand and discern the important voice that was calling him. But with the assistance and experience of the priest Eli, he was able to listen to the Lord and carry out his wishes. By the nature of our own calling, we too must listen, naturally with the help of those charged with our formation and their experiences. We are on the road to discerning properly the voice of the Lord. In a world where there are mounting pressures, becoming alert to the call of the Lord is of absolute importance.

This is more so against the background of the work we are called to do. In the ministry of our Lord, he constantly did battle with the evil one as is evidenced in the gospel reading this morning. Casting out the devil and curing the sick were among the cardinal reasons for the coming of our Lord. It doesn't come to us as a surprise that the whole town came to Jesus to be healed of their ailments. My take on healing is that we as ministers and would-be ministers will continue this work of the Lord if we are able to listen and discern correctly his purpose for us. Many of us have plunged into the ministry without the necessary sensitivity to what it entails. Our Lord shows us the way, and he does it with simplicity and understanding of God's will. At the heart of this healing is prayer. The value of prayer is not to be underestimated in our lives as ministers, for only in a life fine-tuned and built in the discipline of prayer can we be able to courageously undertake in earnest the service of healing. For, it is the Lord himself who carries out this mandate through us. In a world where we are constantly under watch for wrongdoings and the consequence of failures, it shouldn't come as a surprise when we realize that we are told to brace up to the spirits. So a proper understanding of the call of God like Samuel had is important. May we respond to this call with the psalmist in the words of the psalm today: "Here I am, Lord, I come to do your will."[45]

---

[45] Being a homily delivered at the seminary chapel of St. Paul College Seminary, Gbarnga, Republic of Liberia, Wednesday, first week in ordinary time, year 11, January 13, 2010.

The Anointed of the Lord

Joy is a net of love by which we catch souls.
Mother Teresa

DEAR BROTHERS, THE reading this morning provides us the chance again to reexamine very critically and collectively our stands regarding our place in the Lord. We know the unfolding saga between David and Saul, and the redactors of the scriptures ensured that the lesson of the story is captured. We should not by any means or at any point in our lives take it for granted that we can lay hands on the Lord's anointed. This point may be missed by others. It may be overlooked by those who want to impress on the whole world that the anointed of the Lord are just like any other person. While this may look like it is sound, let us be aware and shy away from touching the ones chosen by the Lord. This goes for those who sit and slander, lack appreciation for the efforts put in by those chosen, plot with others to undermine these efforts, and cast aspersions on all the good works of these men and women of God. They should not forget David's borrowed proverb that "Wickedness goes out to the wicked." If you come across those who think they know better than those who have consecrated their lives to the Lord and they are wont to strike, please remind them that the consequences are grave. This is because these are specially chosen.

I say this against a background of the gospel, where the Lord went up the mountain and after prayers called the twelve companions he wanted and chose to be sent out to preach, with power over the devil. It is the Lord who calls. The selection process may be a lot different from today, but we are on the same stake. There are so many cynics, and the world believes that our ministry today is on the verge of decadence. In their eyes, we are not fit for this kind of ministry. Check this out! It is a piece I culled out from somewhere.

The Jordan Management Consultants Group in Jerusalem, to Jesus, Son of Joseph, Woodcarver Carpenter's Shop, Nazareth

Dear Sir,

Thank you for submitting the résumés of the twelve men you have picked for management positions in your new organization. All of them have now taken our battery of tests. We have not only run the results through our computers but also arranged personal interviews for each of them with our psychologists and vocational attitude consultants. The profiles of all the tests are included. You may want to study each of them carefully. As part of our service and for your guidance, we make some general comments, as some auditor generals would include some general statements. This is given as a result of staff consultations and comes without any additional fee. It is the staff opinion that most of your nominees are lacking in background, education, and the professional attitude for the type of enterprise they are undertaking. They do not have a "team concept." We recommend that you continue your search for people of experience in managerial ability and proven capability.

Simon Peter is emotionally unstable, given to fits of temper. Andrew has absolutely no qualities of leadership. The two brothers, James and John, sons of Zebedee, place personal interests above company loyalty. Thomas demonstrates a questioning attitude that would tend to undermine morale. We feel that it is our duty to tell you that the Greater Jerusalem Better Feast Community has blacklisted Matthew. James, son of Alpheus, and Thaddeus definitely have radical leanings, and they both registered a high score on the manic-depressive scale. One of the candidates, however, shows great potential; he is a man of ability and resourcefulness. He speaks well, with a keen business mind, and has contacts in high places. He is highly motivated, ambitious, and responsible. We recommend Judas Iscariot for your controller and right-hand man. All the profiles are self-explanatory. We wish you every success in your new venture.

Sincerely yours,
Jordan Management Consultants[46]

This is the way the world tends to see our choices and maybe the way we see ourselves sometimes. The option and choice to disprove this is available now. We call on the Lord to help us as priests and seminarians in this venture.[47]

---

[46] Tim Hansel, *Eating Problems for Breakfast* (Michigan: Word Publishing, 1988), 194-195

[47] Being a homily delivered at Mass at the chapel of St. Paul College Seminary, Gbarnga, Republic of Liberia, Friday, second week in ordinary time, year 11, 1 Samuel 24:3–21, Mark 3:13–19, January 22, 2010.

Solomon Remarks

A faint faith is better than a strong heresy.
St. Thomas More

S CHOLARS ARE IN disagreement about the wisdom of Solomon, and opinions defer on this issue. Redactors of history and bibliographers have reasons to place within the altars of history their doubts on the wisdom of Solomon. Interestingly, evidence of the arrangement of the courts of Solomon, the building of the temple, and other seminal portrayals of this wisdom, show that he was indeed a man endowed with insight and wisdom. He chose wisdom but was not without mistakes. From a purely priestly account, therefore, the temple edifice and building is enough to qualify that he was indeed a man of wisdom who found favor with the Lord and received his blessings. So in the words of Solomon this morning: The Lord has chosen to dwell in the thick clouds. Yes, I have built you a dwelling, a place for you to live in forever. While scholars contest the wisdom of Solomon, I make bold to state from a concerned student of the Bible that the art of building itself is a wise choice. It carries with it the connotation of a careful assemblage of skilled persons fit to do the job. It requires organization, support, determination, sacrifices, diligence, and above all, skill. If we must build a temple fit for the Lord and requiring the wisdom put in by Solomon, the temple of the Lord that is in our own hearts, then we need to pray to the Lord for the wisdom of Solomon to advance our course. No wonder the gospel reading acknowledges the gifts that this temple of our Lord brings in the person of Christ.

In the Old Testament, God was resident in the temple as exhibited in the clouds, readily available for his people. In the New Testament, Jesus appears, curing all those who were sick. Our world is ruptured in sickness. May the healing touch of Christ repair our damaged souls, heal our land, and restore our dignity. This is my prayer for you this morning and always.[48]

---

[48] Being a homily delivered at Mass at the seminary chapel of St. Paul College Seminary, Gbarnga, Republic of Liberia.

Renounce His Wickedness and Live ...

Faith means battles; if there are no contests, it is
because there are none who desire to contend.
St. Ambrose

T HE PSALMIST IN 130:3 opens up this morning reflection
with a particular contrite question: "If you, O Lord, should
mark iniquities, Lord, who could stand?" There is no better
time than now to reexamine this notion of guilt for the things that we
have done and our need for God's mercy. I am the first in my lifetime
to ask for God's mercy, in the way I have carried myself because every
now and then, I throw out this understanding that there go I but for
the grace of God. Isn't it strange and pathetic that it is the wicked
man who is being upheld in the first reading because of an absolutely
transformative change of heart? He renounces his wicked ways and
sins and turns to the Lord, respects God's laws, and is honest. He will
certainly live. But the honest man who throws away integrity, copies
the wicked man in sin, and practices every kind of filth is not to live
because all the integrity he has shown will be forgotten. He has broken
faith and committed sin. This man will die.

The judgments are immediate and deep or even a harsh, one would
say. "He shall certainly die." The truth, my brothers, is that when it

comes to sin, we must fight a battle to renounce it with all our hearts, minds, and willpower. For sin deals a great blow to man in the sight of God. If we who are human find it so hard to bear with the failings of our kith and kin, imagine what impact our ways have on the reality of God's love. We must reject sin with all the efforts that we can summon, especially at this period of Lent and always. Or else we shall most certainly die. Although it is not the wish of God for man to die, our sin may lead us in that direction. The gospel is very reassuring in the sense that our sensitivity to the needs of the others in our lives is, for me, the passport to heavenly blessing and pride. Once we recollect that we have something against one another, it behooves us to make amends quickly, more so that we daily seek for the abundant blessings of God. There is no room for name calling, stupid jokes, unacceptable gestures, unguided statements, implied judgments, cynical remarks, and, most of all, outright attacks on ourselves. This is the period for real sitting down to take stock of how we have lived and are living, because our efforts at making amends and getting ourselves in the proper disposition are the gift we can give to God and one another in this period of fasting and prayer. Surely, the good Lord, who sees our efforts, will continue to shower us with his blessings, and we shall certainly live. This especially true in the sense that the Lord warns that our virtue should go deeper than that of the Pharisees, who lived with the pretense of the day and compromised on all fronts. May the disease of the Pharisees be far away from all of us who daily seek to do the will of the Lord, and may our efforts be ever more yielding in Christ, who is our Lord and Savior both now and forever. Amen.[49]

---

[49] Being a homily delivered at Mass at St. Paul College Seminary chapel, Gbarnga, Bong County, Republic of Liberia, Thursday, first week of Lent, Ezekiel 18:21–28, Matthew 5:20–26, February 2010.

Nothing by Myself

It is not the actual physical exertion that counts toward
a man's progress, nor the nature of the task, but the
spirit of faith with which it is undertaken.
St. Francis Xavier

TENSIONS AND ANIMOSITY seem to surround us each
passing day. The demands of daily living add to the pressure
of our lives, and the basis for sustenance for others is far more
challenging. However, we are admonished that even if a mother will
forget the baby at her breast or fail to cherish the son of her womb, the
Lord's assurance is he will not forget us. So, in our pursuit of the day-
to-day affairs of life, we may think that we are abandoned, we are alone,
and our efforts don't matter. We may even wonder about the need for
all these sacrifices, if there is any real or imagined reason for them.
Against a bitterly opposing media and an eagerly oriented audience,
the challenges of these times add up to provide real provocation. This
is the story of Lent, where we are to constantly ask ourselves what we
are doing for Lent. The first reading from Isaiah imagines a favorable
time when all this suffering will end and things will be back in shape.
There will be restoration of the land back to its original owners; joy will
overtake the land. This seems to be the thought of the prophet and also
our own thought. As we go through this period, we hope that a time

will come and is almost here when we will be restored back to a more prosperous path that will lead us to God.

This focus is clearly brought out in the challenge of our Lord to the Jews. He can only do what he sees his father doing. At this period, our best teacher and example of the father remains our Lord Jesus in the way he does the things he is doing. If we want to rise with him on that day, then we must learn to work with him on this journey. We must learn to honor him, for he is the source of life. For he reminds us he can do nothing of himself, except the father who sent him directs him to. So, just as we have the assurance from God himself that we are not forgotten at this period of tension and difficulty, we have our paths to him visibly and clearly paved for us by his son, Jesus Christ. Brothers, let us focus again on ourselves, our motifs and conduct, and the place we have of God in our lives. As we do that, let us remember the promises that he has made to us. We are not abandoned in our pains and struggles. In fact, our difficulties are lessened because we know the way to the father. May the good Lord continue to bless our Lenten fast as we prepare for Easter.[50]

---

[50] Being a homily at Mass in the chapel of St. Paul's College Seminary, Gbarnga, Republic of Liberia, fourth week of Lent, Wednesday, Isaiah 49:8–15, John 5:17–30, March 17, 2010.

The Unusual

Do not say that you have chaste minds if you have unchaste eyes,
because an unchaste eye is the messenger of an unchaste heart.
St. Augustine

A CAREFUL AND OBSERVANT look reveals how strange and unusual, our behaviors and actions can be! Nearly every aspect of our lives is a powerful expression of this uniqueness and strangeness. It reveals itself in our environment with distinctive voices and vision. Can one get away with the kind of deep spontaneity and attractive ridiculousness which masquerades itself in our dance, music, feasts, festival and celebrations that almost always pervades us? How about bizarre eccentricities and the narrowness of style as expressed in our fashion, dress code, culinary habits, cuisine, or the arts, and crafts. Think about our unique pattern of movements and architecture, it is mostly passionately adorned with supersonic speed or the unusual happenings around our planet. May I direct you to a few examples of something unusual, which invites creativity and helps us to discover unimaginable potentials and possibilities. I uncovered the Upside Down House, which is really a project created by a Polish businessman and philanthropist named Daniel Czapiewski, and is located in Poland in the tiny village of Szymbark. Worthy of note is rather than simply being a bizarre tourist attraction this house, managed to attract thousands of tourists. It would seem that the house is also meant to be a profound statement about the Communist era and the state of the world. However, the point is "Czapiewski's company would normally take three weeks to construct a house, but this one took 114 days because the workers were disorientated by the strange angles of the walls. Many tourists who visit complain of mild seasickness and dizziness after just a few minutes of being in the structure."

Since, this is about self invention, which is essential and relevant. Here is another compelling story of James Balwin. Before the great writer James Baldwin knew he was a writer and long before he became great! He had the good fortune to meet an artist, a painter, a man who saw something in his young brown face that made him want to open the door and invite Baldwin inside. Walking through that door changed Baldwin's life, opened it up to all sorts of experiences he had never imagined. Baldwin recounts how this painter, Beauford Delaney, often sang Lord open the unusual door. Whether to let someone in or walk through it oneself, at some point in life we all face an unusual door.

This unusual way of living and behavior helps us to see the world differently. It helps to understand people and places, better understand their background and experience and navigate the murky world of their lives. It is that same understanding that can help us understand the mystery behind Mary's annunciation. Perhaps, the understanding Whoopi Goldberg struggled to reach when her fourteen-year-old daughter announced that she was pregnant. What Whoopi wanted for her daughter was not what her daughter wanted for herself. And yet, the fundamental issue was choice. who decides? And how? And what are the consequences? What all of these people experienced in one way or another required them to look hard at the changes they wanted and needed to make in order to better their lives. They had to open up to new ways of thinking, doing, and living.

I dare say that each of our story will be told in a different way, just as each of our life is lived in a unique way. But all the authors share something in common: a willingness to open the door to readers. They invite us in to tell us what happened to them and what they did to make things happen. They let us see who they are, what they think, and how they feel. So consider this introduction a welcome mat, and open the unusual door. You might be letting in a stranger who becomes a good friend. Or you might be letting yourself out to face a brand-new world. Either way, you can't lose. What are you waiting for? Go ahead. Open it. It is extra ordinary one and you are involved in something bigger than you, Hopefully, this can lead to something refreshing and uniquely authentic. Today, Mary choices is no different so unusual so uncertain yet she is the mother of the savior of the world.[51]

---

[51] Being a homily delivered at the chapel of St. Paul's Seminary, Gbarnga, Republic of Liberia, Solemnity of the Annunciation of the Lord, Isaiah 7:10–14, 8:10; Hebrews 10:4–10; Luke 1:26–38, Thursday, March 25, 2010.

Craving for Lasting Things

*For I have learnt for a fact that nothing so effectively obtains,
retains and regains grace, as that we should always be found
not high-minded before God, but filled with holy fear.*
St. Bernard

EAR BROTHERS, AS I prepared to put down a few words for our reflection this morning last night, I was surprised to come across a beautiful piece of literature that caught my attention. I couldn't continue punching the keys of my laptop without a glance at what this writing had to say. It was simply about ways of improving your salaries or earnings. According to the authors, these were just tips to seize up your earning in this difficult financial time. Well, just before you say, "Oh, Donald, not again," just hear me out a little. Our writer had little interesting things to say that made sense for me not in terms of boosting my earnings but rather about helping me to develop tips that are necessary for survival in difficult times. He had things like "Get interested in learning something new," as innovations at these times will certainly help one in a lot of ways. The whole idea of updating what one already knows or improving on the existing knowledge holds well not only for the rewards it will bring to your pockets but to be evergreen and refreshed will add to your fountain of knowledge. These innovations will come when you take the time to find out what is relevant, basic, and understandably available to the nature of job you are expected to work. There may already be existing stereotypes. Others have made advances in labels or the like. But what is really opportune is the fact that at this time we are able to rise above these judgments and excel in what we have set out to do.

Stephen in the first reading today exhibited for me such amazing qualities, and the story is not only well known but the consequences are glaring for all to see. Since he could not be unmatched by those who were perceived to be the opinion leaders of the day, he could not bend with the position of what was obtainable; it was only obvious that he had to go. There was more to this decision because we are told that the men could not get the better of him. Simply put, he showed exquisite knowledge and understanding, but more so, he was filled with the wisdom and spirit of God. What he had were things that will last. As a result, he was not afraid and so could withstand any opposition. The same thing in this period of Easter is what the Lord required of those who were looking for him. Knowing their hearts, he explained that they should crave for lasting things, not only things that would boost their pockets, in this case their stomachs, but things that would carry them through in good times and in bad. This is more so for those of information. Should it not be the case that we should work more for the things that will eventually lead us to God as he had directed, by believing in the one whom he has sent and by putting special emphasis on the prayers we say, the works of charities we carry out, and more of the interpersonal and personal relationships we keep not only with him but with each other? In all honesty, I will be proud to identify with innovations that will keep me more in tune to all that this period offers, and maybe, just maybe, it should begin from nowhere else but from us. As priests and seminarians, we should be leaders in this by believing in the one whom he has sent because we ourselves are also sent.[52]

---

[52] Being a homily delivered at the seminary chapel of St. Paul College Seminary, Gbarnaga, Republic of Liberia, third week of Easter, Acts 6:8–15, John 6:22–29, Monday, April 19, 2010.

Ascension Thursday

Who except God can give you peace? Has the
world ever been able to satisfy the heart?
Saint Gerard Majella

DEAR BROTHERS AND sisters, forty days after the
resurrection, our Lord returns to take his place at the right
hand of God the Father. The ascension of the Lord into
heaven is understood as the final token of Christ's two natures: divine
and human. The accounts rendering the story this morning from the
scriptures are indeed very brief. All synoptic gospels present the events
in a rather brief and specific manner, indicating the mood of the
evangelists and their take on the matter. It was not easy for them to
accept the fact that Jesus had to go back. They wanted him to stay,
knowing that while he was around, his presence was reassuring and
comforting. But that he was going meant a break and looked so distant.
So the disciples became very emotional, and the accounts rendered
here attest to this. However, the reality of our Lord's ascension and his
specific charge to his disciples to preach repentance in his name and be
his witnesses was a task, noble and pure but highly engaging; it required
care and fortification, for our Lord knew he was sending them to a
very challenging task. So the assurance of the Holy Spirit is promised.
This Holy Spirit will cover them with power from above. The gospel
of Mark has it that in his name, they will drink deadly poison and be

unharmed, cast out devils, possess the gift of tongues, pick up snakes in their hands, and lay their hands on the sick, who will recover.

Dear brothers and sisters, we who have been chosen as priests and sisters and those of us preparing for this task have it on the authority of our Lord we are not to remain in the shallow remorse of our Lord's leaving but to be alive with the tasks placed before us, a mission requiring our energy, passion, and resolve, always, knowing that it is the Lord's work. May the ascension of the Lord, which we celebrate this morning, remind us of our responsibilities in a careful preparation for these tasks, which requires being with the Lord in prayer, possessing his spirit, recognizing our limitations, and allowing his spirit to clothe us and show us the paths to follow. As we carry out this mission, may we not think so much of the difficulties we would encounter but be renewed by the promise of being with him forever.[53]

---

[53] Being a homily delivered in the chapel of St. Paul College Seminary, Gbarnga, Bong County, Republic of Liberia, Thursday, May 13, 2010, Year C.

The Duty of Love

Joy is very infectious; therefore, be always full of joy.
Mother Teresa

DEAR BROTHERS, WE have proof of the sufferings of our loved ones and friends, whom the Lord has entrusted to our care. A lot of these difficulties reveal themselves in our interactions with friends, relations, and above all, those under our care. Attempts to explain these worries and difficulties see us classifying these challenges in economics, politics, religion, psychosexual development, and relationships but most of all personal living and relationships with God. We are duty bound, therefore, like the first reading reminds us, to build ourselves on the foundation of our holy faith; we should pray to the Holy Spirit, keep ourselves within the love of God, and wait for the mercy of our Lord Jesus Christ to give us eternal life. These do not seem like plausible answers to one's expectations of instant solutions to one's problems, but to us, it is a duty of love. We recognize that out of love for us, God provides these stages of growth in both prayer and life. No wonder we face these challenges in his love.

We are quick to challenge the authority of God, especially of his son. We would rather avail ourselves of his teaching and love. Even as priests and seminarians, there are times when you possibly feel that this love of God is so distant! You are not sure whether it is the right thing to say or do, which words to pronounce, or how this idea, relationship, or prayer will turn out! Brothers, we all feel this way, like the Jews who challenged the authority of Jesus but would not provide an answer to his question. We all owe God a duty of love. The reason clearly is we may or do not know how? What we know is to radiate this love in all that we do or say—maybe a little kindness here and there, a positive impression on a matter close to one's heart, but most of all, a prayerful disposition that puts God on top of things in another's life. This is how we grow in his love. Let our prayer today be that we may know you and your love for us.[54]

---

[54] Being a homily at Mass in the chapel of St. Paul College Seminary, Gbarnga, Republic of Liberia, Mass for the Blessed Virgin Mary, Saturday, Jude 17:20b–25, Mark 11:27–33, October 29, 2010.

All Sorts of Trials

Charity brings to life again those who are spiritually dead.
St. Thomas Aquinas

T IS VERY prophetic that the reading of this morning draws our attention to all forms of trials that we may have to suffer to prove our faith. These trials will come in all forms. Some may have to undergo fire; some will have to take hot seats and others acid tests. All of these trials are to show that we are worth the quality that we seem to project! For our purpose, we begin our exams. Others may have been undergoing other exams before now, but officially, we begin this week. It is a time when we have to crystallize all that we have been studying in the course of the semester. It means paying more attention, drilling further than usual, and pulling all the necessary strings. No wonder exams are referred to as necessary evils, because although we don't like them, they are so necessary.

The gospel reading today reminds us of the beautiful encyclical of John Paul II of blessed memory, "Veritatis Splendor" (On the Splendor of Truth), where the Holy Father's comments on the rich young man are very illustrative. Our wealth and possessions inhibit our decisions and make us trivialize important matters of truth. One case is denying truths of its important comportment, which is originality and trials. These inhibitions are claims to functional things, instead of quality—the keeping of rules, observances, or regulations and attachments to possessions, instead of detachment that frees, that offers freedom beyond our imaginations. This freedom is in the quality of our upbringing, character formation, spiritual accumulation, and commitment to excellence.

As Jesus reminds the apostles, those who see things with human eyes may envision difficulties, but for those who endear themselves to God and are able to perceive things from his perspective, all things are possible. We commit to this trial that we may undergo as a way of opening ourselves to God so that we will be his forever while praying for your every success in the forthcoming examinations. We submit to a week of trials and difficulties to prove our worth before God.[55]

---

[55] Being a homily at Mass in the chapel of St. Paul College Seminary, Gbarnga, Republic of Liberia.

About the author

D ONALD TYOAPINE KOMBOH, PhD is a priest of the Catholic Diocese of Jalingo, Taraba State of Nigeria. He studied in St. Thomas Aquinas Major Seminary, Makurdi, Benue State, and St. Augustine's Major Seminary, Jos, Plateau State, Nigeria. He was ordained in June 1996. He also holds a master of arts (hons) degree in religious studies from the prestigious Catholic University of Eastern Africa (CUEA), Nairobi, Kenya. At various times in his diocese, he has served as a parish priest, the dean of a deanery, an education secretary, and a member of several commissions of the diocese. He recently graduated from St. Thomas University, Maimi, Florida, with a PhD in Practical Theology. He was an instructor and formator at St. Paul's College Seminary, Gbarnga, Republic of Liberia. Currently, he is the pastor of St. Joseph the Worker Cluster in the Archdiocese of Dubuque, Iowa, and resides in Holy Name Church, West Union, Iowa, United States.